Bendix Field

The History of an Airport and Legendary Pilot Homer Stockert

Quentin L. Hartwig

Schiffer Publishing Ltd®
4880 Lower Valley Road • Atglen, PA 19310

* Photos are courtesy of Ellen Ruppel with the permission of the National Air and Space Museum, Washington, D.C., unless otherwise noted.

Library of Congress Control Number: 2014949921

Type set in Impact/Minion Pro

ISBN: 978-0-7643-4378-0
Printed in China

Published by Schiffer Publishing, Ltd.
4880 Lower Valley Road
Atglen, PA 19310
Phone: (610) 593-1777; Fax: (610) 593-2002
E-mail: Info@schifferbooks.com

Contents

Acknowledgments

The author wishes to thank the following individuals for their contributions and patience in this journey through time.

Air Force Historical Research Agency, Maxwell AFB, Montgomery, AL; Margery Batterson; Catherine Bishop; Carnegie Library, Oakland, PA; Jerry De Munck, Eleanor and Joseph Hayden, William Hite, and Jesse Lewis; Indiana State Library, Indianapolis, IN; H. L. McCombs; Rodger K. Myers, Curator, Greater Fort Wayne Aviation Museum (IN); Doris Pennington, Paul F. Plesnicher; Rita Relue, Defiance Public Library, Defiance, OH; Vicky Rydzynski, Archives/Records Center (for South Bend and St. Joseph County records), South Bend, IN; Jack Saylor; Gertrude Reiner Singer, *South Bend Tribune*; Scott Schuler, Northern Indiana Center for History, South Bend, IN; and to my wife Kathleen, a native of South Bend, for her support, suggestions, and assistance in this endeavor.

I reserve a special thanks for Ellie Ruppel, who allowed me to scan her collection of Homer and Dora Stockert's photographs and memorabilia. That treasure provided the stimulus to continue to acquire more information and photos illuminating the origin of Bendix Field and the creativity of Homer Stockert.

Abbreviations

AFHRA	Air Force Historical Research Agency, Maxwell, AFB,
AL	Alabama
AFB	Air Force Base
CWO	Chief Warrant Officer
1/Lt.	First Lieutenant
2/Lt.	Second Lieutenant
IN	Indiana
NMUSAF	National Museum of the United States Air Force, Wright-Paterson Air Force Base, Ohio
OH	Ohio
PA	Pennsylvania
S/Sgt.	Staff Sergeant
USAAF	United States Army Air Force (same as AAF)
WOJG	Warrant Officer Junior Grade
WWII	World War Two

Foreword

I have been involved with the South Bend Airport since 1968, first as the consulting engineer, then as the staff Airport Engineer, and finally as the Executive Director. I had met Homer Stockert in the late sixties but did not know him well. I knew Dora Stockert well as the astute business woman that she was. Homer was a true aviation pioneer and a legend in his own time. This book sets forth their very real accomplishments during the heyday of aviation. Homer and Dora created the image of the airport to the flying public and it was, and is, a positive one. I am proud to have played a role in the development of the airport and can only hope that it is as well regarded today as it was during the Stockert era.

John C. Schalliol, AAE, PE
Mishawaka, Indiana

Preface

Two institutions came into being separately. Both developed a firm footing, then came together for the common good of the public. Bendix Field served as an aviation center for commercial and private purposes; Homer Stockert advanced opportunities provided by the singular invention of the twentieth century, the airplane.

Bendix Field was the brainchild of an extraordinary entrepreneur, Vincent Bendix. He bought land near his aviation factory to build an airport convenient to his pilots who tested the bounty of aircraft inventions burgeoning from his plant.

At the same time, Homer Stockert gained fame as a young aviator, winning aerial races and demonstrating a genius for using the airplane for tasks unable to perform with grounded vehicles.

In the 1930s, Stockert saw Bendix Field as the airport where he might establish his own identity, his own enterprise, the Stockert Flying Service.

Then WWII inerrupted. Both Stockert and Bendix Field served with distinction. Homer Stockert left the Stockert Flying Service in the hands of his business savvy wife, Dora, and began testing the P-47 Thunderbolt, the heaviest fighter aircraft in the United States Army Air Corps arsenal of front-line weaponry rolling out of the Republic Aviation plant at Evansville, IN. His engaging, managerial personality was quickly recognized and soon, in addition to serving as test pilot, he was named Hangar Operations Manager of Republic Aviation.

Bendix Field served as an important refueling and servicing station for military aircraft crisscrossing the United States toward bases on the North American continent or overseas to theaters of war.

War over, the airport and pilot returned to civilian pursuits. Bendix Field, now recognized as a regional hub for commercial carriers, is referred to as the South Bend Regional Airport.

Stockert returned to his Stockert Flying Service to teach flying, convert military aircraft to civilian applications, test inventions flowing out of Bendix Aviation Corporation, and service private aircraft.

This book hopes to capture the significance of these two journeys.

Chapter 1

From Farm Chores Near Churubusco, Indiana, To Skies Over Fort Wayne, Indiana

Some people are characterized as a legend long after they die, others are so defined long before they die. Homer Stockert's recognition in legendary terms—dean of South Bend pilots,[1] Who's Who among Fort Wayne aviators,[2] and one of the finest pilots in the nation[3]—followed him throughout his extraordinary career as a barnstormer, racer, test pilot, flight instructor, visionary, and manager. He captured the admiration of pilots in the dawn of the magnificent flying machines at the turn of the twentieth century. His skill to capitalize on every advantage a plane could offer will become apparent in the succeeding pages. As the news media highlighted each achievement in the early years of aviation, Homer's exploits made press headlines—a *tour de force*. A study of his life will attest to the truth of such homage.

The Stockert farm, Churubusco, Indiana, where Homer was raised.

Photographed in Fort Wayne, Indiana, Homer expressed confidence with his sister, Lois.

Life for Homer Stockert began on a farm near Churubusco, a community in northeast Indiana. Born May 19, 1899, to Lewis and Grace Stockert, he shared chores with his two sisters, Gladys and Lois. As a preschooler in a three piece suit, Homer and his sister, Lois, were photographed in Fort Wayne, Indiana.

His fascination with flying began as he watched aerial mock combat during basic training near the end of World War I. After completing his military service and returning to Churubusco, he chanced to grasp the controls of a biwing Jenny in 1920.[4] That fateful command captured his imagination and energy for the next forty years.

At age 24, he returned to Fort Wayne to take flying lessons at Wayne Flying Service, Baer Field, in 1923. Earning his pilot's license, he accepted a job as a pilot with the same company. Stockert quickly gained prominence as reflected in the Fort Wayne newspapers, with his success as a racer. Within a few years, he was featured in a "Who's Who Among Fort Wayne Aviators." The article recounted amazement regarding his aerial achievements. It suggested, "Probably no other flyer in this section has hung up such an enviable record as that made by Stockert."[5] The ink had hardly dried on his pilot's license when he was credited with placing first in ten races in various cities in central Indiana.[6] One 25-mile race was held in South Bend, Indiana. Piloting a Travel-air plane powered by the reliable OX5 engine, he placed first with a time of 14 minutes and three seconds, averaging 106.6 miles per hour. His prize was the coveted Studebaker Silver Loving Cup.[7]

Stockert valued the Studebaker Cup and was photographed alone holding the trophy while standing on a wheel of the dependable Travel-air bi-wing. For business promotion, he ordered post cards to be made with the photo. For years, Homer posed in white overalls—sometimes soiled, sometimes freshly cleaned—but always with a smile. That expression

Homer, holding the Studebaker Loving Cup, stands beside the co-owner of the Travel-air plane, Ray Barnett, also of the Wayne Flying Service.

of sociability reflected the essence of his character: friendly, charming, daring, and skilled.

When Stockert was inducted into the prestigious Fédération Aéronautique Internationale May 19, 1928, his required photograph featured him with the same treasured souvenir (see image below).

When not circling race course pylons, Stockert amassed more than 28,000 miles in the air, transporting passengers and goods and instructing students in the art of flying in Fort Wayne.[8] Such

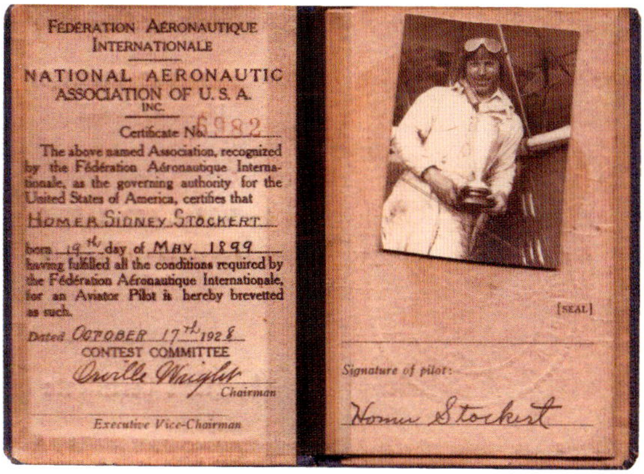
FÉDÉRATION AÉRONAUTIQUE INTERNATIONALE

NATIONAL AERONAUTIC ASSOCIATION OF U.S.A. INC.

Certificate No. 6982

The above named Association, recognized by the Fédération Aéronautique Internationale, as the governing authority for the United States of America, certifies that HOMER SIDNEY STOCKERT born 19th day of MAY 1899 having fulfilled all the conditions required by the Fédération Aéronautique Internationale, for an Aviator Pilot is hereby brevetted as such.

Dated OCTOBER 17th 1928

CONTEST COMMITTEE

Orville Wright Chairman

Executive Vice-Chairman

[SEAL]

Signature of pilot: Homer Stockert

Homer selected the photo of himself holding the Studebaker Loving Cup to be attached to the Fédération Aéronautique Internationale pilot's license. Note that his membership in the prestigious international corps of aviators is validated with the signature of Orville Wright, one of the brothers who flew the first successful flight at Kitty Hawk in December, 1903.

Homer holds the coveted Studebaker Loving Cup he won piloting the OX5-powered Travel-air airplane. The soiled white overalls validated Homer's added talent as a mechanic.

The Fort Wayne Air Museum, located in the Fort Wayne International Airport, is an extensive collection of aviation memorabilia worthy of an afternoon visit. (Photo courtesy of Roger Myers)

exploits in the air landed Stockert in the Art Smith Hall of Fame, located at the Indiana Fort Wayne International Airport.

Before leaving Fort Wayne, Stockert was called upon to fly in honor of Art Smith. After the death of Art Smith—an earlier legendary Indiana pilot—a sculpture was commissioned in his memory. Stockert led a second wave of airplanes overhead during the unveiling of the eight foot high bronze figure located in Memorial Park, Fort Wayne, Indiana.[9]

All this public admiration between 1923 and 1928 did not go unnoticed elsewhere.

Art Smith, an earlier celebrated Indiana pioneer aviator, listed aviators and aircraft aficionados who achieved prominence in the U.S.A., including Homer Stockert. (Photo courtesy of Roger Myers)

Homer's name on the board. (Photo courtesy of Roger Myers)

Chapter 2

A Veteran Pilot, Stockert Sinks Roots in South Bend

A Gain from Fame

Clyde Shockley, "the flying farmer from Kokomo," operated the Rainbow Flying Service at South Bend Municipal airport, South Bend, Indiana. Aware of Stockert's extraordinary range of aviation skills, in 1928, Clyde invited him to become an associate in his Rainbow Flying Service.[1] Stockert accepted the job and immediately created a variety of income-producing pursuits (see photo). In a 1928 photograph, Stockert appears seated on a bi-wing with several aviation enthusiasts ready to carry out any mission.

In 1928, the Rainbow Flying Service offered student instruction and cross country flights. Homer Stockert and fellow pilots flew the Curtiss "Carrier Pigeon," a plane originally designed to carry mail.

How to Make Money with a Plane

The side of a fuselage touted in bold print: "Pilot Homer Stockert Rainbow Flying Service: Waco & Stinson Sales, Student Instructions, Cross County Flights." With an airplane, income could be generated in several ways. In his racing days in Fort Wayne, Stockert once won an impressive $225, out of a total purse of $600 allocated over four races, with cash for two firsts and a 3rd place finish.[2]

The Rainbow Flying Service aircraft rests on a grassy runway at South Bend Municipal Airport, northeast of the city.

Cross country flight could involve the transport of manufactured goods, business passengers, or just a trip around the United States.

Pictures taken from a plane added a new dimension to photography. They could provide the panorama of a fire or accident for a newspaper, aid in surveying, or be sold to an individual or company requesting a photo of their property from above.

Flying cross country could involve transporting merchandise to a distant location. Likely added for the photo op, the banner would be removed before take-off.

Traveling from South Bend, Ind., to the quad-cities by airplane, three South Bend residents, pictured above, attended the dinner last night in Davenport honoring Elmer Layden, director of athletics and head football coach at Notre Dame university. Left to right are: Homer Stockhard, pilot; Jacob Hoffman, president of the Hoffman Hotel system, operators of the Fort Armstrong hotel, Rock Island, and William Sheehan, manager of the Capitol Tire service. They were met at the Moline airport at 4:30 o'clock yesterday afternoon by D. J. McMahon, manager of the Fort Armstrong hotel.

The plane was chartered specially for the trip by Mr. Hoffman. Mr. Sheehan is a close friend of Layden. They were in the same class at Notre Dame, where Mr. Sheehan was captain of the baseball team in 1924. Now Mr. Sheehan is treasurer of the St. Joseph's Valley Notre Dame Alumni association.

For some occasions, Homer piloted in a suit.

The urge to fly quickly mushroomed after the success of the Wright brothers, as an exciting adventure for both men and women. Basic flying lessons, priced at $600, were a major source of income for an aviation entrepreneur. To publicize their student program, Clyde Shockley teamed up with the *South Bend Tribune* to promote an aviation contest for girls. First prize was flying lessons leading to a pilot's license with Stockert as the instructor.

Stockert and Party in Los Angeles to Circle the U. S.

Harry Baker, one of the passengers of Homer Stockert, formerly a pilot here who took off from the municipal airport at Gary on January 22 to circle the United States, in a letter to the News-Sentinel states that the party has arrived safely in Los Angeles. Baker writes that on one occasion they were forced to fly two miles high in order to fly over mountain peaks along the Mexican boarder. Baker's letter is as follows:

"Homer Stockert, flying for the Rainbow Flying Service of South Bend, and formerly of Fort Wayne, has completed part of the flight around the United States and Mexico.

"So far, the flight has been very nice, without the slightest mishap, motor and plane working fine, with the exception of a leaking gasoline tank, which started in New Mexico. The flight being continued to Los Angeles, on one tank, where the other is being repaired.

"Stockert and the two passengers, Joseph Veresh and Harry Baker of Gary and Los Angeles, respectively, were kindly received at all stops. Stops being made at Gary, Ind.; St. Louis, Mo.; Tulsa, Okla., Oklahoma City; Dallas, Houston, San Antonio, Pecos and El Paso, Texas, Lordsburg, New Mexico; Phoenix, Ariz. and Los Angeles, Calif.

"The country and scenery were ever changing, from thickly populated farming country, to the oil lands, ranches, deserts, high Rocky mountains, wild lands along Mexican border, where it was necessary to fly two miles high to clear peaks, and finally beautiful California.

"The flight will continue in a few days, south through Mexico across to Miami, Fla., up the East coast and over to South Bend.

"The flight is being made in a stinson Detroiter monoplane.

ISgden

"Signed,
"HARRY BAKER."

Chartered flights could be to Chicago, Illinois, and back or to Los Angeles, California, and back, by way of El Paso, Texas.

Homer Stockert as pilot and Otto Roach, aerial photographer, are prepared for take-off. Given the size of the camera and the precarious stance of Otto, Homer would prove his piloting expertise as he held the plane steady while maneuvering through sudden shifts of wind.

The photo caption read, "KATHRYN WYLAND won $600 worth of flying lessons in a *South Bend Tribune* contest soon after Stockert settled in South Bend—that was in 1928. While taking lessons, Miss Wyland wrote a series of newspaper articles about her reactions to life in the clouds, and it is still pretty good reading. A promise to make a parachute jump resulted in her death." ("He Taught the Girls to Fly," *The South Bend Tribune Magazine,* February 10, 1957)

More than one hundred applications arrived in the mail. After much deliberation, Kathryn Wyland emerged the winner. She proved to be an excellent selection and quickly earned her wings. She was so enthralled with her experience that she wrote a series of newspaper articles about life in the cockpit. Then tragedy.

She told Stockert she wanted to make a parachute jump, if he would take her up. He later admitted reluctance to do so, but was impressed with her skills. She jumped, but suffered a rough landing; the internal injuries she received led to her death a few days later. This fatality distressed Stockert for years.[2] The only other tragedy to mar Stockert's life was the death of his two-year-old son, Lee Arnold, during a brief first marriage.

Homer Inspires

Jerry De Munck, a veteran test pilot and instructor, remembered his first encounter with Homer:

> One day, my brother Chris took me out to the South Bend airport, north of Mishawaka [Bendix Field was non-existent then]. We decided to take a ride if we could scrape up enough money. That was difficult, but we did. Our pilot was a young guy named Homer Stockert. The flight was made in a Waco 10 with an OX-5 water-cooled engine. Gosh, I liked that ride. So one day soon I meandered back over there myself. Homer spotted me and says, 'You the man who's going to fly?' and I said, 'Sure' and he said, 'Climb in the back seat' and away we went.

Stockert had apparently mistaken him for a new student pilot, but for Jerry, things were never again the same; his flying career had been launched. Several years later, soft spoken but exacting, he joined the Stockert Flying Service as an instructor.[3]

Lewis McCombs: "When I was about 11 years old I built a glider that you held onto and jumped into the air. It did not fly, but I scared the heck out of my grandmother who watched me jump off a tall woodpile trying it out." (Photo courtesy of Mrs. Lewis McCombs)

Another WWII veteran pilot/instructor, Lewis McCombs, recalled his employment at the Stockert facility:

> After obtaining my commercial license, I left Indiana Air Service and went to work for Stockert Flying Service, where I taught ground school to their students. Homer and Dora Stockert gave me enough flight time to obtain my Flight Instructor's Rating and I went to work for them as both a flight and ground school instructor. At this time, we were preparing for the war which had not yet started and our government established the War Training Service and under it, the Civilian Pilot Training Program (CPT) to give flight training to both Navy and Army enlisted personnel, as well as train civilian pilots to become flight instructors. I continued this work and enlisted in the Army Reserve Corps as a private early in 1942, but was not called to active duty, as they considered my flight training job essential. In early 1943, I was called to active duty at the 6th Ferrying Group, Air Transport Command in Long Beach, California.

Lewis McCombs: "My propeller driven 'wind wagon.' My dad gave me the Maytag washing machine gasoline engine. I used a draw knife to whittle out the propeller from a 2 x 4 piece of lumber. It didn't work because the propeller would not stay on the engine." (Photo courtesy of Mrs. Lewis McCombs)

Throughout the years versatile talent gravitated, as shown by McCombs to Stockert. Lewis McCombs's passion for flying began in earnest as a youngster. By eleven he was building gliders and engine mounts to test his propeller design.

While at Indiana Air Service, he started a newsletter (see below), reporting on advancements in aviation, tips on flying, cartoons, jokes, and descriptions of services provided by his employer. McComb served as Editor-in-Chief and drew all the illustrations. Four hundred copies of the monthly eight-page publication were mailed throughout the U.S. and Europe.

Lewis McComb received a Commercial Pilots License at age 20.[4]

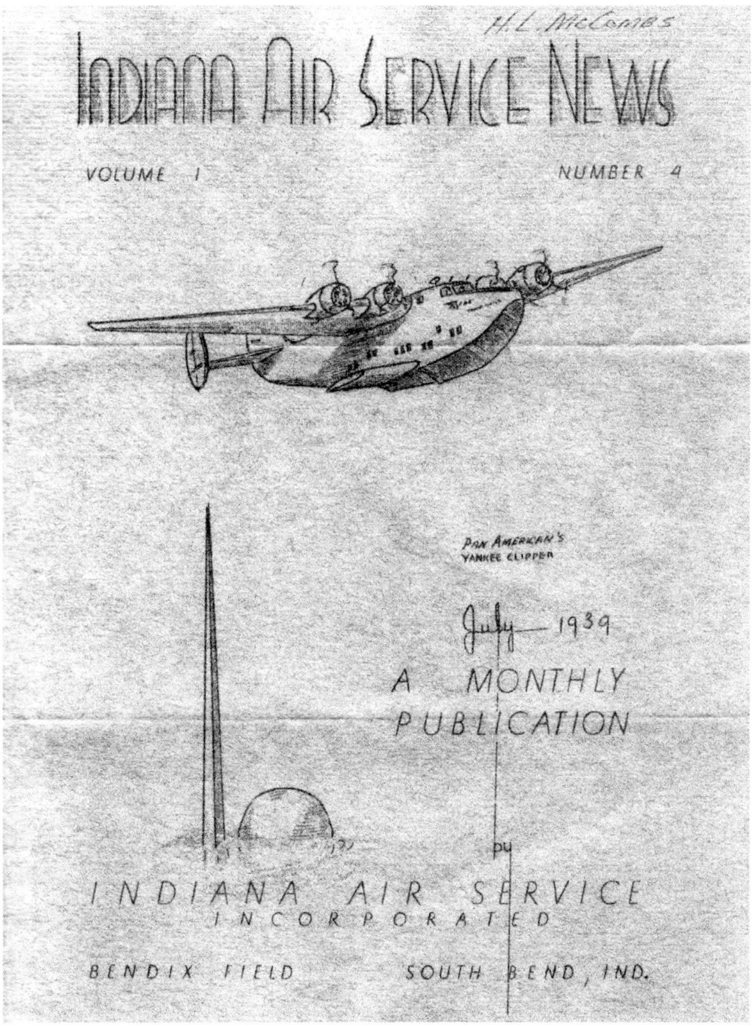

"I had been active in high school with the school newspaper and decided that the Indiana Air Service should put out a newspaper to advertise themselves and also other planes that were for sale. So I started it." (photo courtesy of Mrs. Lewis McCombs)

The Zack Mosley cartoon appeared in 1934, copyright News Syndicate Co., Inc.

Stockert's reputation as a first-class instructor led to a cartoon of him advising a student how to make a landing, should the motor stop.

A brief cash opportunity arose when the huge German *Graf Zeppelin* dirigible motored across northern Indiana, during its record-setting "round-the-world" time of 21 days in 1929. The number of excited civilians wishing to fly near the behemoth far exceeded the planes and pilots available. Stockert flew two lucky passengers, at $200 each, near the motoring spectacle as it soared within 15 miles of South Bend.[5]

Homer flew two passengers close to the *Graf Zeppelin* in a similar airplane on August 28, 1929. (Photo by South Bend Photo Co., South Bend, Indiana)

Stockert generated a subliminal message that flying knows no age or gender limit, when he gave a ride to a ninety-nine year old lady.

The caption read: "'Beats buggy riding all hollow,' said Mrs. Sarah Ribread, aged 99, oldest county infirmary inmate, to Homer Stockert Saturday after a flight from Bendix Airport on her birthday."

Homer Stockert's barnstorming was mentioned in the ancestral file of the Winebrenner Family:

> During this time [between 1932-4], Robert and Jeanie had been able to get a ride in Homer Stockert's open cockpit biplane. He "buzzed" their house. Cora was very upset about this.[6]

By then a veteran of air races, Stockert advised new contestants, such as Lloyd Butz, of the rigors of high speed aerial contests. Unfortunately, Lloyd was killed four years later when his plane and another plane collided in the air near Bendix Field.[7]

In 1933, developments on the west side of South Bend prompted Stockert to eventually strike out on his own. Vincent Bendix, president of Bendix Aviation Corporation of South Bend, had purchased more than 400 acres across town, at Lincolnway West and South Bend's city limits, to build an airport (Bendix Field) for local and transcontinental airlines. Bendix Aviation's research and manufacturing plants would now have a nearby airport where testing of their products could take place.[8]

While still in the process of constructing Bendix Field, Vincent Bendix contracted the Rainbow Flying Service to operate the new airport and offer services currently provided by the South Bend Municipal airport, on the Edwardsburg road, eight miles northeast of South Bend.[9]

Vincent, in cooperation with C. T. Stedman of Rainbow, inked an agreement with Century Air Lines, Inc.—a transcontinental air passenger carrier—to place Bendix Field on their regular schedule. Century even assigned a plane to carry passengers to Detroit in the morning and return them the same day. Such aggressive growth in business spelled the death knell for the northeast South Bend municipal airport.[10]

The popularity of Bendix Field grew rapidly. Notables such as aviatrix Amelia Earhart; Major James H. Doolittle, leader of the famed 1942 Tokyo air raid; and Major Alexander deSeverski, airplane designer, visited the field. The University of Notre Dame football team and coaches flew in and out of the airport.

A new radio directional beam installed at Bendix Field in 1938 improved navigation into the airport. This technology allowed Bendix Field to be classified as an alternate airport for Chicago-New York air traffic. Therefore, should inclement weather prevent airplanes from landing in Chicago, they would land at Bendix Field instead.[11] Bendix Field was fast becoming a field of promise.

The 1933 newspaper caption reads: "Lloyd Butz (right) of Mishawaka, will race this ship in the American Air Races in Chicago today and Tuesday. Homer Stockert, of the Rainbow Flying Service, dean of the South Bend airport pilots, is giving him a few tips before he starts a test hop." (*South Bend Tribune*, July 2, 1933, Section 4, p 2).

Chapter 3

In The Midst of the Great Depression, Stockert Flying Service Emerges

Homer Stockert rode this wave of popularity. When Rainbow Flying Service went out of business in 1933, Stockert purchased its equipment and started Stockert Flying Service to the west of the terminal at Bendix Field. It was a major financial decision during the depths of the Depression, but Stockert was a risk taker. He immediately offered all the services that Rainbow had provided.

Whatever a plane could provide, Homer was ready to offer. His skills were pressed into service on June 30, 1934, when the notorious John Dillinger gang robbed the Merchant Bank, South Bend, Indiana, in a hail of gunfire. With patrolmen and citizens shot in the process, local police sped after the fleeing thieves.

The *South Bend Tribune* paid pilot Homer Stockert to scramble his Stinson Reliant plane and shadow the crooks by air. Officers Levi Nulf and William Million joined *Tribune* reporter Joe Alvin in the lofty pursuit. Despite the horizontal advantage, they failed to spot the gang, because the bank robbers had splintered off into an additional car they had stashed along the way.[1]

In 1936, Homer married Dora Hite, of Ligonier, Indiana. Dora was equally sociable, but possessed a business sense, as well. Her partnership with Homer in Stockert Flying Service developed and she became President of the corporation. She eventually ran the internal affairs of the business while Homer plied his skills in developing and maintaining contacts and contracts for the enterprise.

The municipal airport, northeast of the city on Edwardsburg Road, was incapable of growing with the advancements of the aviation industry. However, improvements to Bendix Field, with Vincent Bendix at the helm, kept pace with the changing times. Stockert Flying Service evolved, too, as opportunities arose. To raise funds, the business was reorganized and incorporated in 1938, with Edward Warren of Three Oaks as a stockholder and officer in the firm. When Warren retired from the business in 1958, Homer and his wife became the sole owners.[2]

Even events in distant worlds had an impact on Homer Stockert.

Chapter 4

Stockert Checks Out The P-47 Thunderbolt For Republic Aviation Corporation In Evansville, Indiana

Duty Calls

On December 7, 1941, the Japanese attack on Pearl Harbor and elsewhere thrust new challenges at the aviation industry. Military aircraft had to be built in large numbers and more airmen had to be trained to fly them. One of Stockert's less promising students was Francis S. "Gabby" Gabreski, who overcame his deficiencies, becoming the top-scoring American ace in Europe by the end of World War II, with 28 aerial victories.[1]

All fighters and bombers had to be tested before being delivered to the armed forces. By September, 1943, both Stockert and Jerry De Munck were testing a P-47 fighter, labeled the Thunderbolt, that was produced at the Republic Aviation aircraft factory in Evansville, Indiana. This responsibility took Stockert away from South Bend for long periods of time,

The Republic Aviation Corporation aircraft manufacturing plant in Evansville, Indiana, was ideally located near a railroad track, for delivery of parts and an air field for testing the famed P-47.

Organized over a vast array of tables, benches, and machine tools, parts are assembled and moved to the production line.

Technicians inspect the power plant of the P-47: a 2,300hp Pratt & Whitney R-2800-59 18-cylinder radial piston engine.

Assembly line for the "razorback" canopy model of the P-47.

Before releasing each new P-47, its fire power was focused for best effect. Eight 50 caliber wing-mounted machine guns pour converging steel into a target.

The P-47 was a killing machine, weighing in at nearly 10 tons loaded, the largest and heaviest single-engine fighter of the war. Colonel Francis Gabreski, WWII European fighter ace, only flew the P-47 in combat.

Scrutiny of the 1943 page of Homer Stockert's flight log book indicates that in the first part of August, in South Bend, as Chief Pilot for Bendix Aviation Corporation, he tested their equipment flying a WACO aircraft. The second half of August and for the next two years, he certified the worthiness of the famous product of Republic Aviation, the P-47 Thunderbolt.

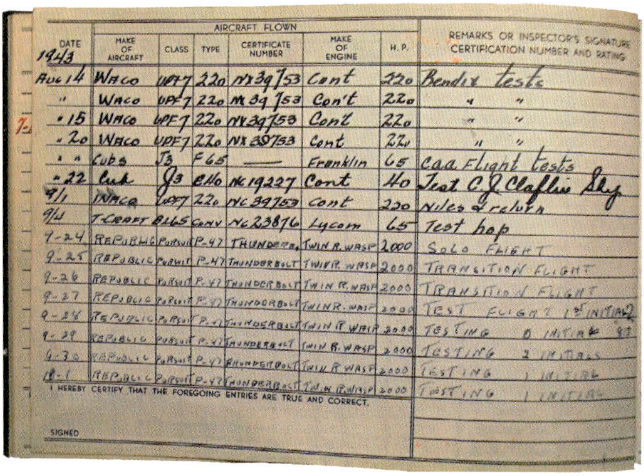

DATE 1943	AIRCRAFT FLOWN: MAKE OF AIRCRAFT	CLASS	TYPE	CERTIFICATE NUMBER	MAKE OF ENGINE	H. P.	REMARKS OR INSPECTOR'S SIGNATURE CERTIFICATION NUMBER AND RATING
Aug 14	Waco	UPF7	220	NX39753	Cont	220	Bendix tests
"	Waco	UPF7	220	NX39753	Con't	220	" "
" 15	Waco	UPF7	220	NX39753	Cont	220	" "
" 20	Waco	UPF7	220	NX39753	Cont	220	" "
" "	Cubs	J3	F65	—	Franklin	65	CAA Flight tests
" 22	Cub	J3	C40	NC19227	Cont	40	Test C. J. Claflin Sky
9/1	Waco	UPF7	220	NC39753	Cont	220	Niles & return
9/4	T-Craft	BL65	Conv	NC23876	Lycom	65	Test hop
9-24	Republic	Pursuit	P-47	Thunderbolt	Twin R. Wasp	2000	Solo flight
9-25	Republic	Pursuit	P-47	Thunderbolt	Twin R. Wasp	2000	Transition flight
9-26	Republic	Pursuit	P-47	Thunderbolt	Twin R. Wasp	2000	Transition flight
9-27	Republic	Pursuit	P-47	Thunderbolt	Twin R. Wasp	2000	Test flight 1st initial
9-28	Republic	Pursuit	P-47	Thunderbolt	Twin R. Wasp	2000	Testing [illegible] initial
9-29	Republic	Pursuit	P-47	Thunderbolt	Twin R. Wasp	2000	Testing 2 initials
9-30	Republic	Pursuit	P-47	Thunderbolt	Twin R. Wasp	2000	Testing 1 initial
10-1	Republic	Pursuit	P-47	Thunderbolt	Twin R. Wasp	2000	Testing 1 initial

I HEREBY CERTIFY THAT THE FOREGOING ENTRIES ARE TRUE AND CORRECT.

SIGNED

leaving Dora to run Stockert Flying Service. She was equal to the task and the business stayed the course through and long after World War II.

Republic Aviation Corporation initially built the P-47 at their plant in Farmingdale, New York. The demand for the P-47 became so great that, on April 7, 1942, Republic broke ground for an additional factory to manufacture Thunderbolts in Evansville, Indiana. Only five months later, on 20 September 1942, the factory produced its first plane, named *The Hoosier Spirit*.

Stockert Tests the P-47—Sometimes It Is Faulty

Homer Stockert joined Republic Aviation as a test pilot in September, 1943.[2] He flew and inspected each new plane coming off the assembly line before approving its delivery to the military. Stockert took his first solo flight in a P-47 on September 24th, and made transition flights the 25th and 26th, as noted in his pilot's log book.

On the 27th, he took a new P-47 up for his first test flight. Each day thereafter, he would test fly one P-47, and sometimes two.

On May 27th, he strapped himself into P-47 #42-28230 at 6:15 a.m., taxied, checking brakes and controls, then took off and routinely evaluated the aircraft in-flight:

> After a thirty-minute check flight, during which the airplane and engine operated normally, including the gear and flaps, I contacted the tower for a normal landing to the south. I made a normal approach, putting the gear down and extending the flaps. The landing gear light was out and everything seemed OK as the ship contacted the ground. I rolled about 500 or 600 feet and the ship had slowed down to about thirty miles per hour. At this point the

Homer Stockert (fourth from the left) joined an elite cadre of test pilots in Evansville to run the rugged P-47 through a series of rigorous maneuvers before approving them for combat. Standing in front of the 12ft 2in four-bladed Curtiss electric propeller, from left to right: Tom Cushman, senior test pilot; James Burke; Perry Bryant; Homer Stockert; Hangar operations manager Leland Roskay; Howard Trunnell; Vic Pixey, chief test pilot; Jesse Gaugh; E. M. McDowell; Gerard De Munck; Ken Ritchey, assistant chief test pilot; and Clyde Putman.

A close up of test pilots standing below Kay Barr while she is sitting on a P-47 (L to R): Captain Bade, Vic Pixey, Tom Cushman, Jerry De Munck, and Homer Stockert. Each pilot wore a flight suit, parachute (hence the straps and buckles), earphones, and a clipboard of flight test procedures attached to their thigh.

The collapse of the left landing gear slammed the whirling propeller into the ground and threw P-47 #228230 into a ground loop. The "bubbletop" was the newest canopy to cover the cockpit.

left wing started to settle, and it continued to do so until it almost touched the ground. The ship swerved to the left, but I held it as much as I could with the right brake.

There was no property damage or personal injury. Damage to the ship appears to be the left wing, left flap, propeller, and engine.

Signed, Homer Stockert, Test Pilot.

An accident investigation determined that the landing accident was due to structural failure of the left landing gear. The damage was repaired.[3] Unshaken by the experience, Stockert was test flying P-47s the next day.

Probably due to the combination of Stockert's congeniality and organizational and piloting skills, he was named "Hangar Operations Manager" March, 1944.[4]

Many held Homer in high regard because of his most appreciated affability and highly skilled capabilities.

The managers stand in front of a P-47 Thunderbolt. Homer's attire was flexible; when executive decorum dictated, Homer looked dapper in a suit, white shirt, and tie.

Homer contemplates his many responsibilities as Hangar Operations Manager, Republic Aviation Corporation.

Homer (on the right) waves to Vic Pixey, chief test pilot, who waves back as he taxies off the tarmac. To reduce drag in flight, the P-47's front wheels folded into the wings, while the tail wheel retracted into a fuselage chamber covered by two flaps.

One of his duties was to serve as a focal point in the investigation of P-47s crashed in the process of being tested. Stockert brought to the job personal experience with aircraft accidents, his own and those of others.

Other P-47 Accidents

At 4 p.m., on August 22, 1944, test pilot Perry F. Bryant took off in P-47 #42-28959 and initiated a series of standard maneuvers. According to his testimony, while he was writing test results the aircraft unexpectedly began to climb; he could not stop the ascent. Suddenly, the plane reversed into a downward spin. Unable to exercise any control, the pilot jettisoned the canopy, released his safely belt, and was thrown from the plane. He parachuted unharmed. Whipped into a flat spin, the plane crashed into a field owned by J. C. Wolfe, seven miles S.E. of New Harmony, Indiana.

An investigation of the crash was immediately implemented. Eight Republic Aviation specialists gave the results of their examination to Stockert, who in turn wrote a summary report and submitted it to the Military Contracts Department. The final report concluded since no structural defect could be found, the pilot may have inadvertently placed the ship into a spin from which he could not recover. No further action was deemed necessary.[5]

Accidents occurred when the pilot in flight paid more attention to writing down test results than to flying. On May 3, 1944, at approximately 8 a.m., two

Homer (right) at the site of an aircraft accident prior to joining Republic Aviation. Nothing was salvageable from that wreckage.

Test pilot Joseph Genovese's P-47 #42-28103 lays in a field about four miles from the Republic Aviation aircraft factory. When the aircraft fell in a flat, horizontal spin, they often remained fairly intact once they hit the ground.

Test pilot Thomas Cushman's P-47 #42-28106 dove into the ground and broke up along a railroad track. Upon burning no parts were salvageable.

P-47s—with Joseph Genovese piloting #42-28103 and Thomas Cushman piloting #42-28106—took off on test flights. At an altitude of 7,000 feet, while the pilots jotted down test results on the tablets strapped to their thighs, Cushman's P-47 drifted toward the P-47 flown by Genovese, and Cushman looked up too late. His propeller tore into the tail of Genovese's aircraft. For a moment, the two planes were locked together, then parted and fell to the ground. Both pilots parachuted safely. Genovese's plane fell in a flat spin into an open field.

Cushman's P-47 broke up and burned when it hit railroad tracks.

The investigation board faulted Cushman's lack of precaution and hinted there may be more to the incident than described by the pilots.[6] Both pilots continued to perform tests.

Among the photos in Homer Stockert's memorabilia is a picture of a wrecked room—probably a kitchen—in a home. "Plane wrecks home" was written on the back. The same picture appears in a March 13, 1944, U.S. Army Report of Aircraft Accident:

Study of this photo in Homer Stockert's memorabilia would conclude someone opened their lunch bucket and was enjoying its contents along with a glass of milk when a plane crashed into the room.

This photo, copied from the old microfilm of the official accident report, shows enough detail to determine it is the same photo present in Homer Stockert's memorabilia. Unfortunately, after all the original photographs of Army Air Force accidents were microfilmed, the photographs were destroyed.

Joseph Genovese, test pilot for Republic Aviation in Evansville, IN, had just taken off in a P-47 at 8:25 a.m. when he lost all power. He described the hopeless dilemma facing him.

> I called the tower for a "crash landing straight ahead" and started to bring the ship down from what appeared to me 150 feet. I first saw the high-tension wires and struck off both switches. After taking out the high-tension wires I saw a house directly ahead and veered to the right, pulled back on the stick, and attempted to lift the left wing over the house and pass the ship between a large tree on the right and the house on the left.

This was the direction test pilot Genovese approached, with the house to his left and the tree to his right. His right wing was sheared off when it struck the tree and is the long white object lying in front of the tree.

I was only partially successful in this maneuver and felt a great shock as the right wing struck the trunk of the tree.

My next recollection was being in the cockpit of the ship on the ground, and I was probably dazed. My first thought was to get away from the wreck, and I crawled out of the cockpit as quickly as possible and started back toward the house when I found that my leg was injured and I had great difficulty in climbing the hill from the position of the fuselage to the house. A young girl ran out of the house with her ear bleeding, and I told her to sit down on my parachute and looked at her ear. Shortly after that people arrived, among them Major Wright and Major Walker.

Later examination of the motor and propeller revealed the mechanism controlling the pitch of the propeller blades had not been properly assembled. Upon take off, the tension of the motor at full throttle sheared the bolts maintaining the pitch, causing the blades to turn flat to the turn of the propeller. Thus, the plane lost forward motion and fell to the ground. The investigation concluded the plane had not been adequately inspected before its maiden flight.[7]

How to Sell War Bonds

The sale of U.S. War Bonds helped raise money to fund the cost of the country's involvement in a global war with the Axis Powers. People of all ages were encouraged to invest in the bonds. Manufacturing plants were prime sites for concentrated potential buyers, Republic included. Periodically, Republic Aviation held Bond sales campaigns, with static displays of the famed P-47 serving as backdrop to girls prepared to sell bonds from booths.

Saleswomen stand ready to sell U.S. government War Bonds and stamps. The small signs at either end of the booths read, "6th War Loan. Republic Raiders Hit The Mark." The famed P-47 Thunderbolt, or "Jug," as it was sometimes referred, stood in the background as a visible reminder of Republic's contribution to the war effort.

War bonds and stamps could be purchased inside the plant, as well. Congenial Homer Stockert had everyone smiling as he signed up for his share.

Another important way employees could demonstrate their patriotism was to show up for work. Employers and employees were proud to announce a low absentee rate. Stockert's smile highlighted the achievement.

Homer Stockert, Hangar Operations Manager, and R. G. Rogers, Factory Manager, shake hands, congratulating the employee team for achieving a low absentee record.

With a few hours free from the rigors of test flying, the Republic Aviation pilots were given a ride in a "ground plane"—the U.S. Sherman tank armed with a 75mm cannon. The pilots were the guests of the Chrysler Evansville Ordinance Plant.

Test pilots were given a brisk ride in the Sherman at its top speed of 29mph, which was the taxiing speed of the P-47. South Bend pilots were Jerry De Munck, (fifth from the left) and Homer Stockert (third from the right).

Sixteen Months in the Air

Largely due to test flying of the P-47, administrative duties at Republic Aviation did not hinder Stockert's continued accumulation of flying hours. By March, 1945, he had passed a total of 12,000 flying hours in his career, which had begun in 1924. Five hundred of those hours were spent flight testing the P-47s built in the Evansville Republic Aviation plant. Stockert calculated those hours by adding up his flying time in six Log Books. Recognizing that few pilots had achieved those numbers in only 21 years of flying, the *Republic Aviation News*, Indiana Division, ran a story highlighting Homer's time in the air. The reporter expressed the accomplishment uniquely:

> To put it another way, that means Indiana Division's hangar operations manager has flown enough hours to keep him up in the clouds for one year and four months without ever coming down.[8]

As Stockert made personal history testing the famed P-47, he temporarily left Bendix Field, an airport with its own unique history.

The caption reads: "With every Log Book he has had since he began his flying career back in 1924 spread out in front of him, Homer Stockert, hangar operations manager, this week added up his flying hours and found he had a total of 12,000. He is shown above as he recorded the last minutes of aviation milestone few flyers can match." (*Republic Aviation News-Indiana Division,* March 9, 1945)

Page Six

P-47 Falcons Win Renown as 'Busi

RAC Fighter, 'Ten Grand,' Joins Unit

Veteran Outfit Has Seen Action in Six Campaigns

When Republic's 10,000th Thunderbolt joined the 79th Fighter Group of the 12th Air Force in Italy it really picked itself a winner! This Thunderbolt group, the 79th "Falcons," has often been referred to as "America's Busiest Fighter-Bomber Side Show," and since the 10,000th P-47 flew its first mission, which was the group's 30,000th sortie, it has taken its place as a veteran in this veteran outfit.

The 79th has been in six campaigns, including: the Egyptian-Lybian, Tunisian, Sicilian, Italian, French, and the Northern Italian. In constant and savage combat this group has flown the roughest, toughest, most perilous of all Air Force assignments — close support, fighter bomber.

In Three Air Forces

The "Falcon" group has flown with three Allied Air Forces — the Desert Air Force, the United States Ninth and 12th Air Forces. During its lengthy combat life, the 79th Fighter Group has flown close support for the ground troops of four Allied armies — the First, Fifth, Seventh, and Eighth —

STOCKERT TOPS 12,000 FLYING HOURS

With every Log Book he has had since he began his flying career back in 1924 spread out in front of him, Homer Stockert, hangar operations manager, this week added up his flying hours and found he had a total of 12,000. He is shown above as he recorded the last minutes of his aviation milestone few flyers can match.

Chapter 5

South Bend's Flighty Approach To Aviation
Coping With A New Concept: The Airfield

A Reason for Being

As the airplane transitioned from a barnstorming, wing-walking novelty to a reliable form of transportation, postal officials began to view aviation as a new means of conveying mail more rapidly across the country. A transcontinental route could be planned to deliver and pick up mail at designated communities. Yet, airfields were lacking at selected sites where planes could land, receive necessary service, and take off safely, with some knowledge of the weather ahead.

On July 27, 1927, representatives of the National Air Transport Company, which held a government contract to fly mail between New York and Chicago, arrived in South Bend by landing on a grassy field at the University of Notre Dame campus. They met with members of the South Bend Chamber of Commerce to discuss a possible location of an airfield near South Bend. The National Air Transport Company route was designed to pass south of the city, so the group visited Nutwood as a site for a landing field. Time was of the essence, as National Air planned to commence flying the route September 1st.[1]

In mid-September, South Bend, still lacking an airport, prompted C. C. Below, manager of the Chicago Flying Service, to admonish: "An example of South Bend's present incapacity to take advantage of air service is revealed in the fact that the Royal Typewriter company cannot land its large plane here and most of necessity, makes its limited delivery by parachute."[2]

A Club Takes the First Step

The St. Joseph Valley Aviation Club broke the impasse by leasing a 230 acre site, from owners William and Mary Matthews, within one-half mile of the paved Edwardsburg road and six miles northeast of downtown South Bend. Aware that the government and air mail contractors required landing fields to be municipal rather than private, the city council voted $18,000 to assume the St. Joseph lease and thus achieve a municipal airfield meeting the legal requirements for air mail contractors. By taking over the lease and not buying the property, the city council retained the option of establishing an airport at another location more favorable to an air mail contractor.[3]

Fascination with aviation events and incidents merited newspaper columns prominently announced on the first page.

One newspaper article proudly asserted that the South Bend Municipal Field was "...fast Becoming Popular with Aviators." On a Monday, a lawyer flew in from Lima, Ohio, to attend a court session.

Nearly five more inches of column was devoted to describing the arrival on Wednesday by plane of H. W. Kempnich, general branch manager of the Becker Roofing Company, for the purpose of meeting with employees at the local store. Mr. Kempnich planned to visit all of the company's 32 branch offices by plane, thus reducing the amount of travel time by 50%. The story pointed out a major saving of time and expense due to the convenience and speed of the airplane, yet all depending on the presence of an adequate landing field at the branch communities. He further promised to return to South Bend in the company's American Eagle plane in time for the official opening. The South Bend Municipal airport opened on May 20, 1928.[4]

Newspaper image caption: "These 10 passengers, two of them pilots of the huge machine, arrived in South Bend Monday morning from Chicago aboard the Stanolind, tri-motored Standard oil Co., plane which will remain here for two days. Reading from right to left: Robert Walton, Mayor Chester R. Montgomery, Harry Elmore, Charles Wagner, Leslie Morehouse, George O'Brien, Knute Rockne, Mrs. J. L. Phelps, Pilot R. S. LaMont, Pilot J. L. Phelps." (*South Bend News-Times*, April 24, 1928:4.)

Adequacy of the municipal field was demonstrated when the "huge" tri-motor Stanolind passenger airplane landed there, bringing in ten passengers.

Mayor Chester R. Montgomery and football coach legend Knute Rockne were among the dignitaries.[5] Their trust in flying strengthened the public confidence in the roles of aviation.

The YMCA responded to local boys' interest in airplanes by holding model airplane contests in the YMCA gymnasium. Every boy in St. Joseph County was eligible and could build a rubber-band powered plane, with suggestions from adults at the Y. One hundred youngsters filed entry papers for the event.[6]

Entertainment of the Day: Air Shows

The first air meet held at the South Bend Municipal airport was sponsored by the St. Joseph Valley Aviation Club. The front page article on May 18, 1928—appearing the Wednesday prior to the Saturday and Sunday meet—reported that more than 30 planes—one fropm as far away as Lansing, Michigan—would compete in a variety of contests. Capping each day's event would be an awesome exhibit of airport lighting illuminated by nine million candle power, through a revolving beacon and floodlights.[7]

A feature in the air show event would be the crowning of the "Queen of the Air." One entrant featured in a photo article, named Adele Hutchinson, was known to be a frequent visitor to the South Bend airport with the hope of flying her own plane some day.[8]

On Saturday, the first day of the event, the crowd watched between showers as several airplanes raced around a 25-mile course. The reporter marveled how daring the pilots flew close to the ground as they rounded the pylons. Farnam Parker, the winner of the event, was only 16 years old, competing with veteran aviators twice his age. Parker's first place won him the Oliver Hotel Trophy. Homer Stockert placed third. Walter Kysor, a Niles, Michigan pilot, left the race due to an error. Later, he won the "dead stick" landing, when he landed his plane closest to a given spot with motor turned off and wheels without brakes.

Mayor Chester R. Montgomery participated in the dedication of the field as South Bend's Municipal Airport and crowned Miss Betty Osborn "Queen of the Air." That night, the crowd was thrilled with a display emitted by multimillion-candle-powered floodlights.[9]

The second day of South Bend's first air show was equally entertaining. More than 20,000 spectators arrived by automobile, clogging the roads, which took hours to clear. The weather was more accommodating as the crowd watched a parade of airplanes, parachute jumpers, and two minor accidents. Willis Kysor, flying in a 25-mile course, flew too low, resulting in his undercarriage being torn off when it hit a mound of dirt. He managed to land safely.

A valve in the motor of a giant Ford air cruiser tore loose, causing the plane to lose power. The pilot managed to land the distressed airplane in an open field two miles from the municipal airport. Young Farnam Parker, who the day before won the 25-mile race, dazzled the crowd with stunts at high and low altitudes.[10]

Building on the enthusiasm shown by the public for the first air show, the St. Joseph Valley Aviation Club held a second air show only four months later, on the 15th and 16th of September, planned to be more spectacular than the first. Intent on avoiding the traffic jams of the first show, the Assistant Chief of Police supervised the efficient flow and parking of throngs of automobiles. For the first time in South Bend history, United States Army planes flew into its municipal airport. They arrived shortly after noon from the Wilbur Wright Field, Dayton, Ohio, to the cheers of thousands of spectators.

During the day, entertainment was provided by races, parachute jumps, stunts, clown acts, and music piped-in through an elaborate amplification system. In the evening, some forty fliers who performed during the day, many from neighboring states, were invited to watch the movie "The Lights of New York" at the Colfax Theater. The Colfax had received the film "Movietone News," with sound, by air mail just a few days earlier.

The following day (Sunday), 30,000 persons attended the air show, which featured a variety of races and stunts by nearly fifty airplanes throughout the day. A photograph in the *South Bend Tribune* showed many planes parked along the edge of the field, enabling the crowd to get a close look at that new phenomenon, the airplane. M.V. Aavang, the winner of the free-for-all race, left the other contestants behind, as his plane managed a top speed of 130 miles per hour. Among the judges of the aerial events were Donald Eldredge, South Bend World War I ace, and Mayor Chester R. Montgomery.

A curious accident occurred with a pilot who intended to participate in the weekend events. An eleven-year veteran army pilot, Lieutenant O. O. Niergarth, commanding officer of the Army fliers from Wright Field, landed safely Saturday, but fell ill and remained in his room at the Oliver Hotel all day Saturday. Feeling no better Sunday morning, he attempted to experience some fresh air by leaning out his fifth floor window. Unfortunately, he leaned too far and fell two floors into a skylight that stopped his fall. He suffered a broken wrist, numerous cuts and bruises, and possible internal injuries. Captain Rinehart, a medical officer from Wright Field, flew to South Bend to attend to the injured pilot.[11]

Enter A New Player in the South Bend Airport Saga: Entrepreneurial Vincent Bendix

Although the St. Joseph Valley Aviation Club and the city council highlighted the municipal airport on Edwardsburg Road with popular air shows, public attention shifted to a new South Bend airport, with the opening of Bendix Field three miles northwest of the city, May 1, 1931. Vincent Bendix's genius was his ability to recognize deficient auto and airplane parts and either acquire companies that produced

From right to left: Vincent Bendix; Will Rogers, famed humorist; George Freyermuth, Mayor of South Bend; and John T. McGovern, sports writer/editor for the *Minneapolis Journal*. Bendix, legendary tycoon of South Bend, was a genius of mechanical invention and attainer of lofty goals. Achievement of his goals was enabled by his flamboyant attraction of influential personalities. (Identification of individuals by Angie Kindig, The Archives, The University of Notre Dame, Notre Dame, IN; photo courtesy of the Center For History, South Bend, Indiana)

superior products or invent them himself. Auto and plane parts were built at the Bendix plant, located northwest of downtown South Bend.

To test these products, in early 1929, Bendix purchased 410 acres of land just a mile and a half away, near Lincolnway West highway. He converted the land into an airport and wooed Rainbow Flying Service away from the Municipal Airport to manage the new airport. Rainbow had leased three of the four hangars at Municipal and their departure caused that field to wither away.

The new airport boasted runways, a new hangar office complex to house both Bendix and Rainbow personnel, and a day/night lighting system. A 100-foot driveway connected the field to Lincolnway West. Bendix Field officially opened for business May 1, 1931.[12]

The popularity of Vincent Bendix was obvious at the dedication ceremonies of Bendix Field, September 5, 1933. Prominent aviators and public officials streamed into South Bend that day to participate in the christening of the field as Bendix Municipal. Present were winners of the transcontinental Bendix Trophy Races: Maj. James H. Doolittle, Capt. Jasper H. Haizlip, and Roscoe Turner, in 1931, 1932, and 1933, respectively.

In 1930, Clifford Henderson, promoter of the National Air Races, convinced Vincent Bendix to fund the first transcontinental air race. Already owning plants producing airplane parts and not one to miss the opportunity for national recognition, Bendix organized the first Bendix Trophy Race in 1931 with a purse of $15,000. Four entered, with Major Jimmy Doolittle taking first place with a win of $7,500. (Photo courtesy of the Center for History, South Bend, Indiana)

Also present were German WWI ace Lieutenant Ernst Udet, noted aircraft designer Major Alexander deSeverski, and others mentioned in the newspaper accounts. Internationally famous explorer Admiral Richard Byrd telegrammed that he would build an airport at the South Pole and name it Bendix Airport. Mayor W. R. Hinkle performed the christening ceremony in the presence of 20,000 spectators.[13]

Vincent Bendix Exhibited Unusual Patience on this Deal

Even before Bendix Field opened May 1, 1931, Vincent Bendix offered the field to the South Bend city officials at a cost less than his investment in it. The city began steps for the acquisition, but found they lacked sufficient bonding power to buy the field. Negotiations dragged on, and by 1936, Bendix shook the lethargic bargaining by threatening to move his manufacturing plant out of South Bend. Threatened by the loss of jobs and a significant impact on their tax base, the city of South Bend finally bought the airport for "the paltry some of $193,000."[14]

Wartime aggression in Europe and Asia eventually swept the United States into World War II. Previously hesitant, the United States rose to the occasion by mounting a huge war-time production of military goods, including airplanes. South Bend's Bendix Airport lay in the path of military planes streaming across the United States and therefore became a servicing station for the thirsty aircraft.

Chapter 6
The Army Air Corps At Bendix Field

A Requirement During Global Conflict

World War II brought a whole new buzz to Bendix Field. Two decades after the Wright Brothers' historic flight in 1904, the awe and excitement of the airplane slowly diminished. Only aerial races, daring stunt pilots, and wing walkers sustained the allure of powered flight. A dastardly assail on a peaceful nation propelled the airplane to a new place in the American experience.

The attack by the Japanese air force on Pearl Harbor and other U.S. installations in the Pacific region transformed American industry into an arsenal of democracy. From 1941 to 1945, factories ground out every sort of combat weaponry for the U.S. military and for the Allies, as well. Every month a new record number of aircraft, tanks, guns, etc., were produced and transported to where they were most needed.

Fighters and bombers, which were usually flown to their destinations, required gas stations along the way. Thus, military aircraft were crisscrossing the United States in every direction, from factory to modification centers to the front. Bendix Field, already a commercial airport for a decade, was a logical selection as a military refueling, maintenance, and respite site for thirsty fighters and bombers.

Bendix Field Goes to War

Prior to World War II, three intercontinental airlines—United, American, and Transcontinental and Western (TWA, later Trans World Airlines)—provided passenger service to Bendix Field. Initially, United and TWA landed there only when Chicago's O'Hare airport was closed due to inclement weather. By December 1941, the routes of both United and TWA were amended to include stops at South Bend.[1]

The airport covered 320 acres and was one of the ten largest in the United States.[2] In 1940, the terminal sat back from the hangar area at the edge of a taxi strip leading to the runways. Atop the building, an

Aerial photo of the terminal and hangars present at Bendix Field in 1939. The terminal (A) was positioned back from the hangar line. (Photo courtesy of *South Bend Tribune*)

air traffic control tower enabled the controllers to see over the hangars to direct the movement of airplanes at the airport. That year, three military planes landed at Bendix Field, providing a glimpse of what would arrive for maintenance once the World War II factories began churning out thousands of aircraft for the war effort.

The Bendix Field terminal before it burned down February 6, 1942. The caption to this photo read: "Airline arrivals and departures were posted outside the airport's administration building in 1940." (*South Bend Tribune*, April 8, 1990.)

The Douglas B-18 Bolo in this picture resembles the B-18 that landed at Bendix Field. In answer to Army Air Corps specifications for a bomber, Douglas modified its DC-2 into a bomber. The two-engine aircraft was first delivered to the Army in 1937. Many were destroyed during the Japanese attack at Pearl Harbor. It was replaced by the Boeing B-17. The B-18 was modified to hunt enemy submarines. (Photo courtesy of NMUSAF)

The P-36 Hawk, manufactured by the Curtiss-Wright Corporation, served as a front line fighter for the United States from the mid-1930s to the beginning of WWII. It was flown in combat by the French Air Force against the Germans in 1940. The P-36 was the predecessor of the Curtiss P-40, which saw extensive combat for the United States in WWII. The newspaper caption read: "The late-model P-36-A army fighter ship shown here on a taxi strip at Bendix field, St. Joseph County Airport, landed at 10:45 a.m. Saturday from Chanute Field, Rantoul, Ill. One-half hour later a B-18-A bomber from Chanute field landed with Lieut. R. W. Ryder and Lieut. P. H. Dane at the controls. It carried 10 army student fliers as passengers. After picking up a rubber mat made by the Mishawaka Rubber & Woolen Manufacturing Company, the two ships took off at 12:23 and 12:25 p.m. for Chanute field. In the photo are H. W. Otto (left), station manager for the American Airlines here, and Lieut. Ryder. Lieut. Carl Swyter, who flew the P-36-A was not at the field when the picture was taken of his ship." (*South Bend Tribune*, March 31, 1940)

A Curtiss P-36 fighter and a Douglas B-18A bomber landed at Bendix Field March 30th. Both aircraft arrived from Chanute Field, Rantoul, Illinois, in the morning and left for Chanute early afternoon.

A Boeing B-17 Flying Fortress on a navigation training flight flew into Bendix Field June 20th non-stop from March Field, near Riverside, California. Accommodating such a four-engined bomber demonstrated the capacity of the field to handle the largest of aircraft in the United States's aerial arsenal.

Fortress Flies Here From California in 7½ Hours.

Most imposing visitor at the South Bend airport today was this army air corps Boeing flying fortress that flew nonstop 1,758 miles from March field, near Riverside, Calif., to South Bend in seven and one-half hours. Much of the flight was at altitude of 24,000 feet where the crew had to use oxygen. Some idea as to the size of the four-engine bomber can be obtained by comparison with the men beside it. It landed here early this morning after a celestial navigation training flight and took off again after a four-hour stay for Selfridge field, near Mt. Clemens, Mich. Members of the bomber's crew, some of whom are shown about the craft, are Capt. W. R. Morgan, in command; Capt. J. S. McBeth and Second Lieut. H. T. Wheless, both navigators; First Lieut. R. B. Stith, Sergts. H. K. Hunsberger and Stanley Modzeleski and Private First Class W. J. Bendig. The huge ship found accommodations at the South Bend airport more than sufficient for its needs.

The Boeing B-17 Flying Fortress served throughout WWII in both the European and Pacific theaters as a heavy bomber. (*South Bend Tribune*, June 20, 1940)

On February 6, 1942, the terminal was destroyed by fire. This disaster created an immediate problem for the three passenger airlines; they lacked a terminal where passengers could conduct the necessary transactions or wait for their flights. Not waiting for the city and county officials to construct a new terminal, the three transcontinental airlines built a temporary terminal. R. L. Dobie, Vice President of Eastern Operations, United Airlines, wrote a letter to the War Production Board, Washington, D.C., imploring them to grant the county commissioners permission to build a permanent terminal.[3]

Configuration of Bendix Field

Government aerial and employee ground level photographs provided a panoramic view of South Bend's military and civilian airport in the mid-1940s. On 320 acres just off Lincoln Way West (Route 20), four long runways crisscrossed the field in front of

July 23, 1945. 1. Indiana Air Service, 2. Terminal and Military Complex, 3. Stockert Flying Service, 4. Entrance to the airport from Route US 20. The compass headings of the two major runways are identified by capital letters. (Structure identification by Jack Saylor, photo courtesy of National Archives, College Park, Maryland, Box 165, RG 18, 385R-21)

Aerial photograph taken of Bendix Field on July 23, 1945, when the Allies had won the war in Europe but were still fighting the Japanese in the Pacific: A, The civilian-military complex; B, military offices; and C, Homer Stockert Flying Service. The paucity of buildings surrounding the airport is proof of its existence in the countryside outside South Bend. (National Archives, Box 165, RG 18, 385R-23)

July 23, 1945. 1. Indiana Air Service hangars, 2. Indiana Air Service office and restaurant, 3. Maintenance facility, 4. Military complex, 5. Fire and Rescue building, 6. Air traffic control tower and terminal, 7. Wind indicator tetrahedron, 8. Entrance to the airport from Route US 20. 9. Civilian conservation corps barracks served as temporary quarters for the army personnel until the Military complex (4) was completed (Structure identification by Jack Saylor). (National Archives, Box 165, RG 18, 385R-24)

a military/civilian complex. In orderly fashion, the buildings were laid out east to west on the south edge of the field. The temporary air traffic control tower and terminal built by the three airlines servicing South Bend certainly fit the description temporary and somewhat tacky. Jack Saylor, who worked for United Air Lines from September, 1945, to November, 1950, remembers the building very well:

> The so-called tower was only three stories (approximately 30 feet) tall. It was a rather flimsy six-sided wood frame

Circa 1944. A Storage shed owned by St. Joseph County is to the left of the three-story air traffic control tower (center). The first floor of the tower was the office of the airport manager, the second floor was the office of the tower chief, and the third floor was air traffic controller's operations. To the right of the tower is the passenger terminal. (Photo courtesy of Gertrude Reinders Singer)

Circa 1946. Three United Airline employees stand on a loading ramp in front of the Bendix Field Air Traffic Control Tower (from left): Jack Saylor, Ronald Cooper, and station manager Brentano Anderson. Compared to the photo at left, this was taken about two years earlier; some modification of the top floor of the tower had been made, and some shrubbery was planted near the terminal. (Photo courtesy of Jack Saylor)

and siding structure. It was so cheaply constructed that when sustained winds approached sixty miles per hour or more it had to be temporarily evacuated. However, it was equipped with up-to-date radio and navigational equipment. The personnel were also well trained professional Air Traffic Controllers and Weather Bureau employees.

The passenger terminal was equally rudimentary, as Jack Saylor described it:

> This miserable excuse for a passenger terminal was built and owned by the three airlines serving Bendix Field: United Air Lines (UAL), American Airlines (AA), and Trans World Airlines (TWA). Each of the airlines conducted their operations out of one room approximately 12' x 20', with a ticket counter and baggage scale out in front. The rooms were side by side from north to south: UAL, AA, and TWA. A small lobby about 20' x 20' was located to the west of the airline ticket counters.

A DC-3 standing on the tarmac in front of the Bendix Field terminal in 1945; a loading ramp has been fitted to the passenger door. American Airlines demonstrated their support of the war effort by having the phrase painted "Buy War Bonds" on the tail. (Photo courtesy of Joseph Hayden)

Saylor recalled that the engines on the DC-3 and DC-4 were prone to catch fire when started up. Should such an event occur, an employee standing nearby with a fire extinguisher would douse the flames.[4]

Circa 1944. Passengers inside the airliner must have felt some trepidation seeing an employee standing outside ready with a fire extinguisher should an engine catch fire. (Photo courtesy of Gertrude Reinders Singer)

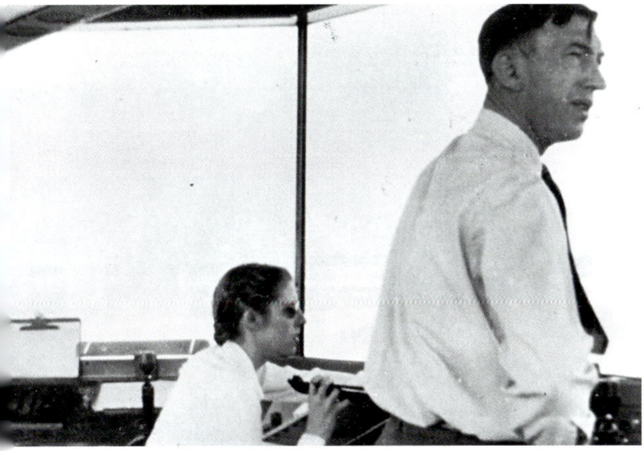

Controller Trudy Reinders works with Luther (Skeeter) Dillon, Tower Chief, in the Bendix Tower in 1945. Other controllers were Larry Morton, Albert (Doc) Essex, Arned Eide, and Eugene Smith. (Photo courtesy of Gertrude Reinders Singer)

Four of the first six female air traffic controllers at Bendix Field were (from left): Gertrude (Trudy) Reinders Singer, Dorothy King, Eleanor Hall, and Edna Gilbo. Other women controllers were Marge Rabe and Mary Edith Kern. (Photo courtesy of Gertrude Reinders Singer)

Woman Air Traffic Controllers

World War II depleted the workforce as men were swept into the services. Women were drawn into positions usually held by men because the war effort depended upon all citizens. Gertrude (Trudy) Reinders attended a ten-week Air Traffic Controller course in Chicago, Illinois, offered by the Civil Aeronautics Administration (CAA). Since she excelled, CAA retained her in Chicago to help instruct new trainees. This, plus time in the Chicago Midway air traffic control center, prepared her for a permanent position in the Bendix control tower in late 1943. Trudy joined three other women and worked with controllers maintaining ground-to-air duties around the clock.[5]

Wartime at Bendix Field

Prior to the arrival of an Air Corps service contingent, in October 1942, First Lieutenant F. D. Ely of the Army Air Corps and Robert F. Bratton, Manager of the St. Joseph County Airport (Bendix Field), surveyed an area of Bendix Airport suitable for the Army Air Corps servicing facilities. The area selected included a sheet metal hangar with an earth floor, leaky roof, a lighting system, and a telephone. The survey document described the area selected, the hangar and its condition, which could be referred to in the event "any controversial question concerning the physical condition of the property when released by the Government." On August 8, 1942, the Army leased Bendix Field and its facilities from the St. Joseph County Board of Commissioners for $1.00 per annum."[6]

On July 13, 1943, two officers and 20 enlisted men in a convoy of two trucks, one ambulance, and two personal cars arrived at Bendix Field from Romulus, Michigan. Captain William E. Dillon was in command and Lieutenant Norbert R. Schenk was the Executive and Engineering Officer. They replaced a Servicing Detachment from the Fairfield Air Service Command comprised mostly of civilians.

The new unit, called the First Ferrying Service Detachment, took complete control of military aircraft servicing at Bendix Field August 1, 1943, when the last of the Fairfield Detachment moved out. The new unit occupied the hangars and shops formerly used by the Indiana Air Service at the east end of the field. Air Corps supplies, Quartermaster, Post Engineer, and Fiscal activities would be provided by the 820th Army Air Force (AAF) Specialized Depot located in South Bend, Indiana.

Allied victories in WWII demanded rapid changes in the United States to keep abreast of new requirements by the military. The changes in the army designation and personnel at Bendix Field were chronicled in the Unit Histories of the 570th AAF Base Unit. The First Ferrying Detachment was upgraded to the First Ferrying Service Station on February 22, 1944, then redesignated the 570th AAF Base Unit on April 1, 1944.

The Revolving Personnel Door

Warrant Officer Junior Grade (WOJG) Wilbur L. Peshia arrived December 17, 1943, and was appointed Adjutant. On February 15, 1944, 1/Lt. Willie Pennington arrived to become Operations Officer. 1/Lt. George M. Weibel was transferred from Billy Mitchell Field, Milwaukee, Wisconsin, on April 19, 1944, and was designated Adjutant. WOJG Peshia then assumed the role of Supply Officer. Three months later, on July 31, 1944, Lt. Weibel was transferred to Easter Sector Headquarters staff, Columbus, Ohio, and was replaced by First Lieutenant Cecil H. English.

A year after he arrived at Bendix Field, Captain Dillon was transferred and Captain Lloyd M. Graves assumed the role of Commanding Officer. On June 21, 1944, Captain Graves was promoted to the rank of Major.

First Lieutenant Schenk was transferred to the 3rd Ferrying Group, Romulus, Michigan, on August 7, 1944, and was replaced by First Lieutenant Arling H. Johnson, who assumed the duties as Engineering Officer. Lt. Pennington was also assigned to the 3rd Ferrying Group and replaced by Captain Edward G. Pickett, who became the Operations Officer.

Second Lieutenant Joseph P. Poist arrived September 17, 1944, to replace WOJG Peshia, who left for the 2nd Ferrying Group, Wilmington, Delaware. Captain Pickett was assigned to the 5th Ferrying Group, Dallas, Texas, on October 31, 1944, and his duties as Operations Officer were taken over by Lieutenant Bert M. McMillin.

First Lieutenant John V. Budukiezicz arrived December 16, 1944, as Assistant Operations Officer. One month later, he was transferred to the 3rd Ferrying Group, Romulus, Michigan.

Captain Laurnace W. Frierson arrived from the 20th Ferrying Group, Nashville, Tennessee, on January 16, 1945, to become Operations Officer. Lieutenant McMillin then became Assistant Operations Officer.

Chief Warrant Officer Paul F. Plesnicher transferred from the 2nd Ferrying Service, Greensboro, North Carolina, to Bendix Field on February 15, 1945, to become Adjutant, thus relieving Lieutenant English, who was transferred to the 2nd Ferrying Station, Greensboro, North Carolina.

Functions of A Ferrying Station

American aircraft factories produced prodigious quantities of all types of military planes that needed to be ferried across the country to distant war zones. Across the U.S., thirsty aircraft needed efficient handling before they continued on their journey. Despite the frequent turnover of personnel within the AAF unit at Bendix Field, the many Army, Navy, and Marine aircraft landing—986 alone in June, 1944—received expert servicing. This included gasoline refueling and oil if necessary, pre-flight check of all aircraft, and maintenance, including engine changes if needed. The field operated around the clock, with an alert crew ready for any service requirement.

The Bendix base provided all the basic living necessities for both permanent personnel, as well as transient pilots and passengers. Dining and housing facilities were present near the flight line at the Military Complex. Trucks and private vehicles were available to transport individuals and goods to and from the base.

The Operations Office provided the essential command and information enabling the base to operate efficiently. A large blackboard listed the incoming and outgoing aircraft. An area map displayed any danger and restricted areas that pilots should be aware. Data from the weather station enabled pilots to chart their course as free as possible of inclement conditions.

Daily Activities of Military Personnel As Reported by the 570th AAF Base

June 1944

In addition to their servicing duties, airplane and engine Air Corps mechanics engaged in on-the-job training essential to promotion. A list of 141 projects was scheduled to be completed before an increase in military grades could be granted. A total of sixteen mechanics were present for servicing purposes around the clock.

Several officers and enlisted men were promoted, but a radio operator on a transient C-60 transport learned the consequence of being tardy; he failed to be present when his C-60 took off June 4th. He remained on base until June 7th, when he was returned by train to his home base as requested by his Commanding Officer. His reception at home base likely cured him of further dilatory behavior.

July 1944

Pilots at the base logged 44 hours in administrative and transport flights in July; there were 2 UC-78s and one L-5 permanently assigned to the base for such purposes. During the month, 600 ferried military planes were serviced. Twelve remained until replacement parts could be obtained.

The surface of the aircraft parking area was sod. During dry periods, taxiing aircraft or planes whose motors were being tested there created large clouds of dust. Such a condition made servicing

UC-78. Produced by Cessna and called the Bobcat by the Army Air Force, the aircraft was used primarily as a personnel carrier. Its maximum speed was 175mph. (Photo courtesy of NMUSAF)

The L-5 Voyager was built by the Stinson Division of Consolidated Vultee. A light aircraft, its major roles in WWII were as an artillery spotter and air ambulance. The two-seater was unarmed and constructed of steel tubing, plywood, and doped cotton fabric. (Photo courtesy of NMUSAF)

aircraft by mechanics very unpleasant. Therefore, whenever possible, servicing and parking aircraft were conducted on the taxi strip.

August 1944

The monthly report highlighted the promotion of several enlisted men: Robert A. Donham, Sergeant to Staff Sergeant; Louis M. Guillemette, Corporal to Sergeant; Raymond C. Marano, Corporal to Sergeant; Sherwood Slate, Corporal to Sergeant; David L. Johnson, Private First Class to Corporal; and Stewart S. Parker, Private to Private First Class.

Beside the probability of being transferred after a short stay, any newcomer to the base had to master and carry out a variety of responsibilities. When 1/Lt. Cecil H. English arrived at the base August 2, 1944, he assumed the duties of Claims and Legal Officer and Provost Marshal, as well as "numerous other assigned duties."

Special note was made of the transfer of 1/Lt. George M. Weibel from Bendix Field to Columbus, Ohio. As Adjutant of the 570th at Bendix Field, he performed other duties, such as Legal, Personnel, Classification, Signal and Communication, Provost Marshal, and Special Services Officer. Judging from his popularity, he performed these many duties with distinction and won the praises of both officers and enlisted men. They all wished him well in his new advanced assignment. The unit history credited his sound and fair decisions as a major contributing factor for the high morale at the base; such high morale within the 570th was mentioned in numerous unit histories. In the months reported, there were no instances of AWOL (Away WithOut Leave), nor the need of a stockade. The Fifth Service Command film library maintained a steady supply of films for the entertainment of off-duty men.

A major factor in the high morale was the food served at the Mess. A cook named Cpl. Bernard E. Burkey was one who carried on the "traditions of our mess hall for good and wholesome foods properly prepared."

Several men left on furlough: Corporal Marvin D. Macy, Sergeant Richard F. Flanegan, Private William T. Nelson, Private Paul H. Brady, and Staff Sergeant Oral Pratt.

On average, each day twenty military planes arrived for servicing and left. They ranged from fighters, such as the P-63; P-40s; trainers; and bombers like the Consolidated B-24 Liberator, the B-25, and Navy planes.

September, 1944

An inspection team from the Eastern Sector conducted their periodic review of policies and duties. Their report indicated the unit was operating efficiently. The unit previously obtained ordinance supplies directly from Camp Atterbury, Indiana. The procedure was changed so that supplies had to be ordered through the 3rd Ferrying Group, Romulus, Michigan. The unit found this added routing of requests caused inefficiency in their daily operations.

Service personnel who returned from overseas duty for furloughs and leaves were assigned to military installations closest to their homes; many came to the 570th at Bendix Field for the necessary paperwork. The unit history proudly described their efficient handling of the necessary filing of reports that detained the service men or women usually less than an hour when they were eager to return to their families. Many returning officers and enlisted men were temporarily assigned to the 570th.; therefore, the Morning Report of those present could range from a normal 67 men to 110 to 130.

One segment of the ongoing education of personnel at the 570th was the use of precautionary devices to prevent venereal disease. Instruction was frequent in order to keep sick time to a minimum. The request for such material remained secret, so that the user did not have to fear such activity might be held against them during decisions relative to furlough, promotion, and duties. Another factor in the high morale at Bendix Field was attributed to the casual relationship between officers and enlisted men. Officers did not "pull rank" and furloughs were granted when due.

October 1944

An accident occurred when 570th flying officer Captain Pickett was approaching Bendix Field in a UC 78; he clipped a high tension wire about half a mile out. Fortunately, he landed safely with his passenger, Lieutenant Johnson. The only damage was to the props and wings.

A party was held for the officers and enlisted men with a special invitation to those civilians in the area who had contributed to the welfare of the personnel at the base. Major Graves, Commanding Officer of the 570th, played an important role in supporting the organization of the party.

First Helicopter to Land at Bendix Field

On November 14, 1944, the first helicopter landed at Bendix Field. The ship was one of the first purchased by the Army and the flight was considered experimental. A supply truck had followed the helicopter and only arrived at the base after the helicopter landed.

Several high-ranking officers visited the base this month. On November 9, 1944, Assistant Secretary of War for Air Robert A. Lovett and Major General M. S. Fairchild landed after being denied landing in Chicago due to bad weather; they were driven to Chicago by car. On the same day, Vice Marshall S. R. Howsom, Royal Canadian Air Force, and party were also forced to land due to inclement weather. L. C. Bresson, Special Assistant, Office of the Chairman, War Production Board, Washington, D.C., landed due to mechanical problems. When Bresson returned to Washington, he wrote a warm letter of commendation to Lt. Arling H. Johnson, thanking him and his servicemen for their prompt servicing of his airplane. Col. Robert M. Love, Deputy Commander of the Ferrying Division, and party landed for an informal visit on November 11th.

December, 1944

Bendix Field was pummeled by numerous severe winter storms. Despite the drifting snow and icy conditions, the runways and taxi strips were kept clear, making landings and take-offs as hazard-free as possible. No accidents occurred due to field conditions. Commercial airline pilots landing at the field remarked that the conditions at Bendix Field were better than other fields between Chicago and New York City. Because of weather conditions, many military and commercial aircraft bound for Chicago landed at Bendix Field. However, due to the excellent road and rail connections between South Bend and Chicago, passengers could get to their destination by land despite weather conditions.

Another inspection was made of the base. The conclusion was that, with few exceptions, the 570th base unit performance was favorable.

January 1945
Commander Holds Party for His Troops

This last available monthly unit history reflected the same high morale as noted in previous unit histories.[8] In the beginning of the month, Major Lloyd M. Graves, commander of the 570th, held a gala party at the Indiana Club that was attended by three hundred officers, enlisted men, and guests. Support of the event came from Pulaski Post No. 359, American Legion; the *South Bend Tribune*; Bendix Local No. 9, U.A.W.; George Wyman and Co.; Robertson Bros. Department stores; and Gilbert's Men's Store.

> A floor show featured a group of entertainers from the South Bend Shriner club under the direction of Herald Fites. A barbershop quartet consisting of Dr. Clarence O'Dell, Joseph Bella, George Corbridge, and Stanley Katmirski sang several numbers. A local soloist was Sgt. Richard Flannagan, of the local base. The show opened with a baton twirling act by Margaret Smith, while the Air Commandos, an orchestra from Baer Field, Fort Wayne, Indiana, played the Air Force song.

The Commandos played music for dancing and WSBT, the *Tribune*'s broadcasting station, broadcasted the orchestra's music.[9]

The broad segment of attendance and local business and civic support of the party attested to the working military and civilian relationship between the Army Air Force units at Bendix Field and the South Bend population.

Bendix Field was honored with a short visit by the leading war ace of the United States, Major Richard Bong. His record of 40 Japanese shot down in the Pacific Theater was the best of all the U.S. combat pilots. He was greeted by Major Lloyd Graves, commandant of the 470th while a 15° F light snow fall prompted the conversations to be congratulatory and brief. He then continued his flight in a United Airlines passenger plane to Chicago, then on to Popular, Wisconsin, his home town. The newspaper article also included a picture of his bride to be, Miss Marjorie Vallendahl, shown baking bread in anticipation of Major Bong's arrival.[10]

On July 27, 1945, the *South Bend Tribune* carried a photo of the mayor with commanding officers of the different army units stationed in South Bend. Mayor F. Kenneth Dempsey is shown signing a declaration proclaiming the following Wednesday as "Army Air Force Day." Behind him was Major F. D. Ely, commanding officer of the 820th A.A.F. Specialized Depot, 1217 South Walnut Street; Lieutenant W. J. Pennington, acting commanding officer of the Air Force unit at Bendix Field; and Lieutenant Colonel Harold H. Beebe, A.T.S. City Plant representative.[11]

Mayor Urges City Mark Air Force Day.

Trib 7-27-45

Mayor F. Kenneth Dempsey has proclaimed next Wednesday as "army air force day," and requested that all South Bend observe it as the 38th anniversary of the founding of the corps. From small beginnings, Mr. Dempsey pointed out, the force has been built into the most powerful fighting air command in the world history. Shown in the picture as the mayor issued the proclamation are, left to right, Major F. D. Ely, commanding officer of the 820th A. A. F. specialized depot, 1217 South Walnut street; Lieut. W. J. Pennington, acting commanding officer of the air force unit at Bendix field; Mayor Dempsey, and Lieut. Col. Harold H. Beebe, A. T. S. C. plant representative.

—Photo by Tribune Staff Photographer

This photo with caption appeared in the *South Bend Tribune,* July 7, 1945.

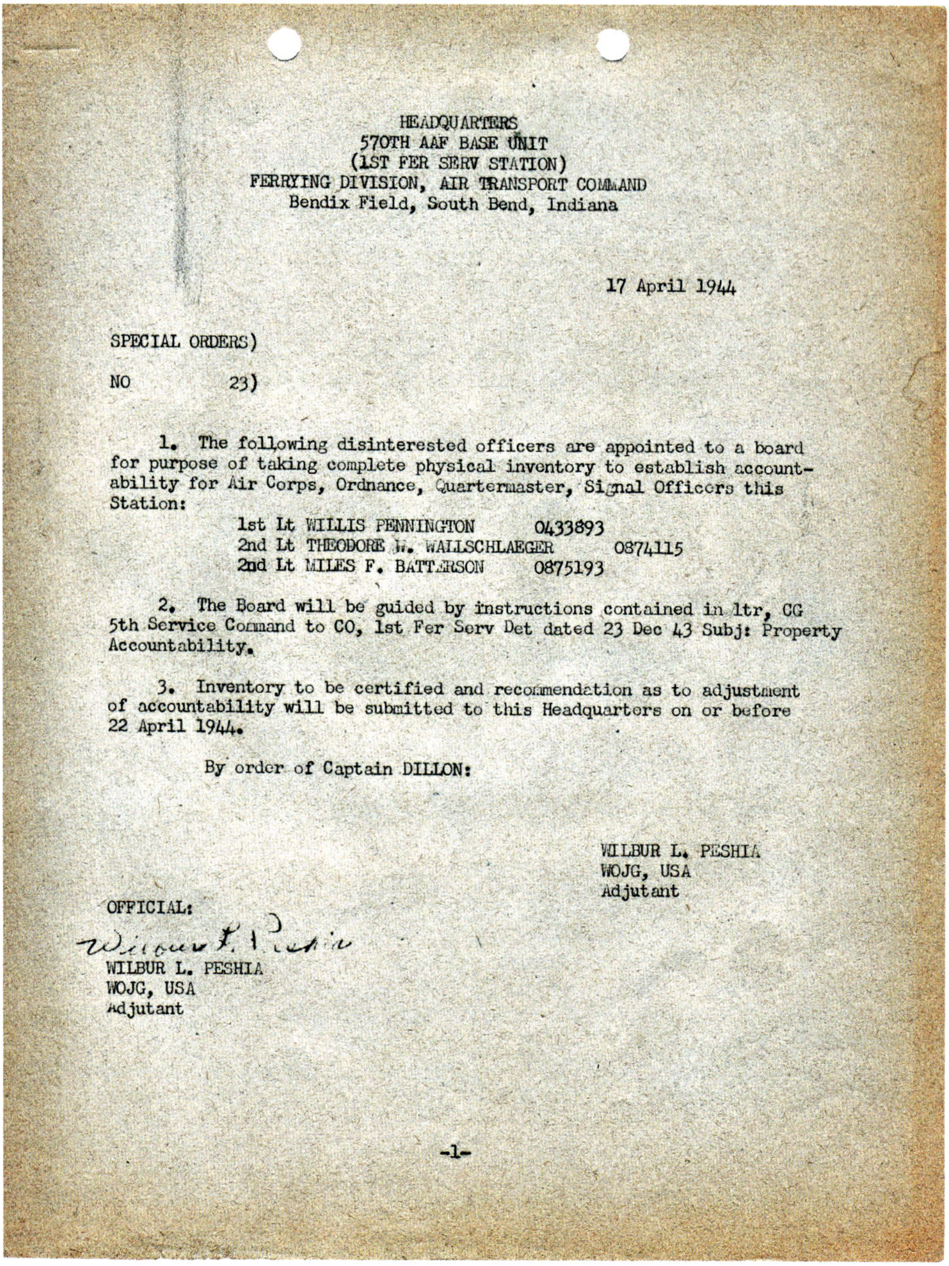

HEADQUARTERS
570TH AAF BASE UNIT
(1ST FER SERV STATION)
FERRYING DIVISION, AIR TRANSPORT COMMAND
Bendix Field, South Bend, Indiana

17 April 1944

SPECIAL ORDERS)

NO 23)

1. The following disinterested officers are appointed to a board for purpose of taking complete physical inventory to establish accountability for Air Corps, Ordnance, Quartermaster, Signal Officers this Station:

1st Lt WILLIS PENNINGTON 0433893
2nd Lt THEODORE W. WALLSCHLAEGER 0874115
2nd Lt MILES F. BATTERSON 0875193

2. The Board will be guided by instructions contained in ltr, CG 5th Service Command to CO, 1st Fer Serv Det dated 23 Dec 43 Subj: Property Accountability.

3. Inventory to be certified and recommendation as to adjustment of accountability will be submitted to this Headquarters on or before 22 April 1944.

By order of Captain DILLON:

WILBUR L. PESHIA
WOJG, USA
Adjutant

OFFICIAL:

WILBUR L. PESHIA
WOJG, USA
Adjutant

-1-

Stationary of the 570th AAF Base Unit verifying its presence at Bendix Field. (Military Order courtesy of Mrs. Margery Batterson)

Comparison of Leases

That same day, the *South Bend Tribune* carried an article noting the beginning of the closing down of the Air Force servicing unit at Bendix Field. U.S. Senator Raymond E. Willis informed the *South Bend Tribune* that beginning August 20, 1945, the unit would be reduced to a caretaking operation of about twenty men. The skeleton crew enabled the army to maintain a presence at $1.00 per annum, should international conditions require returning to a full contingent. Efforts by the aviation commissioners to obtain increased rent from the army beyond the $1.00 per annum were never successful.

More than a year before, the Civil Aeronautics Administration (CAA) assumed operation of the control tower and equipped the tower with additional instruments. As the Army Air Corps terminated their presence at Bendix Field, the CAA would do the same. The financial responsibility of maintaining the control tower would fall to the county commissioners, who did not have that cost, operator salaries, and replacement instrumentation figured into their budget.

Bendix Field was an inexpensive ride for the Army Air Corps, which leased the airport, including the Indiana Air Service facilities, for $1 per annum; the county commissioners were responsible for the maintenance of the field and the buildings erected by the Corps were of temporary construction, thus of little value.

As previously mentioned, the St. Joseph County Board of Commissioners leased Bendix Field to the Army Air Corps August 8, 1942. A year later, the St. Joseph County Board of Aviation Commissioners traveled to Fort Wayne, Indiana, and learned, to their dismay, the profitable lease the Fort Wayne commissioners had negotiated with the Air Corps. Fort Wayne purchased 728 acres of land for $125,000 during February 1941, which the Corps leased, then invested more than $7,000,000 to build a huge air terminal that would become, at no cost to Fort Wayne, the property of Fort Wayne when the Corps vacated the field. The field, known as Baer Field, was maintained at the Corps' expense. In comparison, the St. Joseph county commissioners and the Works Progress Administration (WPA) spent about $1,300,000 in capitol investment and several hundred thousand dollars in operating costs during the Corps' presence at Bendix Field.[7]

Chapter 7
Army Facilities in South Bend Support Bendix Field

AAF Weather Station at Bendix Field

In February 1944, because of increasing military air traffic across the continent, the Army Air Corps Ferrying Division decided Army weather stations should be established at South Bend, Indiana; Rochester, Minnesota; and Fargo, South Dakota.

The South Bend Weather Bureau, already present at Bendix Field, was primarily an observation facility without the capacity of forecasting weather. A forecast capability across the Midwest had become essential due to inclement weather patterns that hampered speedy delivery of military aircraft from factories to modification centers and overseas installations. Forecasting would enable control towers to divert pilots around troubled weather patterns as they ferried aircraft to their destinations. Such forecasting would also be advantageous to commercial airlines and private pilots.

Initially, space to accommodate the forecasting unit was limited to sharing the office of the Weather Bureau at Bendix Field. In February 1944, Lt. Theodore W. Wallshlaeger, a forecaster, arrived at Bendix Field to establish the Army Air Corps forecasting unit. He was soon joined by two more forecasters: Lieutenant Miles F. Batterson on April 1, 1944; and Lt. Edgar E. Martin on May 28, 1944. Their efforts led to the official designation of the unit as the Bendix Field Weather Station May 1, 1944.

As the Army Weather Station grew in personnel and equipment, it was necessary to find a separate room. Lieutenant Wallschlaeger shared this problem with Major Graves, commandant of the 570th AAF unit at Bendix Field, who sympathized with the issue and arranged for the Weather Station to be installed in the Pilot's Lounge located in the Operations building. Such accommodation was only adequate when storage space was made available in other buildings.

Lieutenant Wallschlaeger constructed a scale model of the room to arrange the best location of the desks, display counters, and equipment. The move from the civilian Weather Bureau to the Pilot's Lounge was completed on August 16, 1944.

Numerous personnel changes were noted. Sergeant Lester R. Wilderman, fresh from the forecaster's school for overseas returnees at Chanute Field, arrived October 1, 1944. On October 2, 1944, Staff Sergeant Charles E. Powers was transferred out to the base hospital at Baer Field. Private First Class Earl E. Richter was transferred to Spring Lake, New Jersey, on October 13, 1944. Although their loss diminished the observing staff, they were replaced the following week with two new observers: Private Alfred C. Fournier and Sergeant Monroe E. Schwimmer.

In November, Lieutenant Carroll J. Miles left on the 30th and Lieutenant Edgar E. Martin was ordered to Morrison Field, West Palm Beach, Florida, December 28th. These changes left the station with four forecasters: Lieutenant Wallschlaeger, the Station Weather Officer; Lieutenant Charles C. Surland, Tech Sergeant; Earl J. Barrows, the station chief; and Sergeant Lester R. Wilderman. The three observers were Sergeant Monroe E. Schwimmer, Corporal Howard E. Snoke, and Private Alfred C. Fournier.

The unit history recognized that the forecasters, coming from different training centers, did not receive the exact same education. Therefore, all new forecasters would serve on a shift with a veteran forecaster as an informal on-the-job training. A buck slip attached to all new correspondence was required reading for each new shift. Once each member had read the attached documents that person would initial the buck, indicating he was up to date on new information, then pass the document on. Each weekly meeting, a different forecaster would present information on new developments in the field. These procedures provided the best possible means of maintaining a technically efficient air force forecasting station at Bendix Field.

The forecasting station shared its weather information with the Kingsbury Ordnance Plant, LaPorte, Indiana, and the 820th Specialized Depot, South Bend, Indiana, enabling both outside units to plan their travel knowing future weather conditions.

Quarters for the enlisted men were provided in the GI barracks on base. Officers lived off base, as no quarters existed for them. All military personnel ate in the field mess hall. Food was available around the clock, since the field was open on a 24-hour, seven-day week schedule. By all reports the food was satisfying, a factor contributing to the high morale at the base. Major Graves, Commanding Officer of the field, with support of South Bend businesses, held numerous parties for all personnel at the field.

The First Three Months of 1945

The weather station received an additional teletype machine so new that the Western Union installers had to learn new procedures as they put it in place. Lieutenant Wallschlaeger, known for his ingenuity, established a "squawk box" for communication between the Army weather station and the civilian South Bend Weather Bureau.

Changes in the personnel continued with usual rapidity: Private Alfred C. Fournier left for the Weather Equipment School, Spring Lake, New Jersey; and Sergeant Monroe E. Schwimmer joined the weather station at Kearns. Staff Sergeant Charles Neimeyer and Corporal Justin Vranek arrived from Stout Field as observers. Late January, Sergeant Harry W. String reported for duty (as the unit history observed as a pun)—all six feet of him! On the first of March, Corporal Wesley Winter arrived to increase the number of forecasters, only to be transferred five days later.

Both Lieutenant Wallschlaeger and Sergeant Barrows attended Forecasting Seminars at different weather training stations. The men were nervous during a technical inspection, but all went well and few corrections had to be made. In March, Lieutenant Wallschlaeger was transferred to Lunken Field, and he would be remembered for his able command and ingenuity during his tour at Bendix Field. Lieutenant James T. Donahue, however, arrived to take his place as a forecaster.

April Through June 1945

This last weather station unit history noted continued improvement of weather displays for ferrying pilots. Large area maps included weather conditions over the Great Lakes, enabling the pilots to plot the best course to their destination around troubling weather conditions.

Incoming personnel during the quarter were Tech Sergeant Sylvester Solodyna, forecaster; and Staff Sergeant Fraser and Sergeant Fred Hanes as observers. Departing were Tech Sergeant Earl J. Barrows, Sergeant Lester R. Wilderman, Sergeant Harry W. String, Staff Sergeant Fraser, Private First Class Buerosse, and Private First Class Berger.[1]

The 820th AAF Specialized Deport, South Bend, Indiana

Insight of the operations of the 820th Depot could be gleaned from their available unit histories. On March 5, 1943, Major H. J. Brown, Headquarters, Fairfield Air Service Command, Ohio, traveled to South Bend to ascertain the feasibility of establishing an Army Air Forces Depot in the Oliver Farm Equipment Company Plant No. 2 at 1217 South Walnut Street, South Bend, Indiana. The survey concluded that the plant would serve the needs of the Command, so Major Brown was ordered to activate and command the 37th AAF Storage Depot in Plant No. 2.

Major Brown's first task was to arrange the necessary structural changes and repairs necessary before supplies were shipped to the depot. The unit history identified six buildings (Buildings #101 to #106) that needed a variety of changes and repairs before they could be used. With the assistance of Captain Foster D. Ely of the Bendix Field AAF Ferrying Service Detachment, Major Brown coordinated with Mr. Stolte and Mr. George Lanphere of the Oliver Equipment Company to identify and assign to the plant those Oliver employees who could operate and maintain the mechanical equipment in Plant No. 2. Mr. Medland, the local Civil Service representative, was asked to identify skilled and semi-skilled personnel to serve at the plant as crane operators, truck drivers, and takers on other tasks necessary for efficient operation of the Depot. Mr. Clare Pittman, local director of the Defense Housing Corporation, was asked to arrange housing for the many individuals brought to South Bend to work in the plant.

On May 25, 1943, the first shipment of equipment arrived at the Depot. Much to the dismay of the Depot Commander, many requested items were either missing or in a number far below that requested, making operations difficult.

The lease between the Oliver Farm Equipment Company and the United States of America was signed June 1, 1943. The unit history identified several people who held administrative positions at the Depot:

Norman E. Luginbuhl, Administrative Assistant
Orville B. Hankins Supervisor, Misc. Supply
Ellen H. Hankins Personnel Section
Harvey Higginbotham Supervisor, Class 07 (Paints & Dopes)
Thomas J. Brannigan Supervisor, Class 06-B (Aircraft Lubrication Oil)
Douglas D. Parsons Supervisor, Class 24
Larry Forgy Supervisor, Class 12 (Fuel and Oil Dispensing Equipment)
Helen Morris Basic Administration
Esther Manning Clerk, Class 07 (Paints, Dopes)
Jessie Bell Transportation
Donna Gibson Clerk, Class 24

The Personnel Section at the AAF Servicing Detachment at Bendix Field was absorbed into the Personnel Section of the 37th AAF Storage Depot

This exterior sign designated the purpose of the facility: the 820th Army Air Forces Specialized Depot. The sprawling building was located at 1217 South Walnut St., South Bend, Indiana. (Call: 206.820-1V.2; IRIS No. 143322, AFHRA)

The warehouse was leased from the Oliver Farm Equipment Company of South Bend, Indiana. Skilled personnel from the Oliver Company were retained at the warehouse by the Army Air Corps to operate and maintain the various electrical and mechanical installations within the facility. (Call: 206.820-1V.2; IRIS No.; 143322, AFHRA)

for efficiency reasons. By December 1, 1944, 476 civilians were employed at the Depot.

The 37th was redesignated the 820th AAF Specialized Depot on August 4, 1943, in General Order 33, dated August 5, 1943, from Headquarters, Fairfield Air Service Command, Patterson Field, Fairfield, Ohio.[2]

As the war favorably progressed into 1945, the 820th was plagued with absenteeism, likely due to the idea that the war was practically won and thus workers could take some time off. Major Foster D. Ely, the new commandant of the 820th, believed otherwise and initiated a plan to instill more patriotic fervor in the employees. The plan was called "Presenteeism." Ely organized the workers into teams and each day identified the team with the greatest percentage of workers on the job. Hopefully, the workers would take pride in being on the team with the highest percentage and thus show up for work. Major Ely believed any slacking of efficiency "at home" could negatively affect the men and women on the battlefields.[3]

Chapter 8

Postwar Stockert Flying Service

The Japanese surrender to the Allies September 2, 1945, on the battleship USS *Missouri*, in Tokyo Bay, sharply curtailed the production of the P-47. Stockert's last test flight in the Thunderbolt, powered by a 2,800hp engine, was September 13, 1945. Returning to South Bend, the next dozen flights were in aircraft with a horsepower of 450 or less—a major change in horsepower, but not in personal drive. Back to work at the Stockert Flying Service in peace time was not slow time for Homer. The nation was playing catch up, with civilian pursuits stalled in deference to tasks necessary to win the war. Homer and Dora aimed to provide all the services the varied customers sought. Despite his

Date taken: July 23, 1945. A. Terminal and Military Complex, B. Stockert Flying Service, C. Entrance to the airport from Route US 20 (D). The compass headings of the major runway are identified by capital letters. (Structure identification by Jack Saylor, National Archives, Box 165, RG 18, 385R-21)

lengthy absences from his flying service while testing at Republic Aviation, his corporation survived, despite the restrictions of WWII.

After the war, the GI bill fueled a surge of interest in flying lessons by the Civil Air Patrol (CAP), military reserve pilots, and civilians. Both Stockert Flying Service and the Indiana Flying Service at Bendix Field possessed state and federal accreditation to offer aviation courses, so many returning veterans sought flying lessons; Stockert offered day and night ground school courses at Central High School, South Bend, with H. Lewis McCombs in charge of the program.[1]

Aerial photograph of the Stockert Flying Service taken on July 23, 1945. Upper left is convergence (1) of airport entrance and Lincoln Way West (US 20) (2). The Stockert office (3) is building to left of hangars. To right of hangars (4) the small white building (5) was the original office but then used for storage. An aircraft is taxiing toward a runway and one aircraft stands between the two hangars. (National Archives photo no. 18-AO-R385-25)

Close-up of the Stockert office and hangar in the mid-1940s. The front of the hangar advertised Standard Oil Products. On the later modernized hangar seen on page 72, the advertisement shifted to Shell.

As a dealer of Cessna airplanes, Stockert also captured the cost of their maintenance, hangaring, and repair.

Given the high interest among returning GIs and the continued fascination with airplanes by the general population, the press closely covered any aviation news, including availability of the flying courses. "Mr. Stockert said his service is authorized to give private, commercial, commercial refresher, instructor, single-engine and multiengine rating course while Indiana Air service offers largely the same courses except for the commercial and multi-engine ratings."[2] Stockert is credited with instructing more than a thousand students.[3]

Stockert employed a crew of five full-time Civil Aeronautics Administration (CAA) licensed mechanics and kept them busy maintaining privately-owned aircraft parked at the Stockert hangars, as well as the planes used in flying instruction.[4] In 1947, Stockert opened a dealership for the Cessna Aircraft Company. His salesmanship was rewarded in 1972, when Cessna presented the Stockert Flying Service with a plaque in appreciation for 25 years of continuous service as a Cessna dealer. The presenters of the plaque were Cessna's Chairman of the Board and the President.

The new hangar. Caption of the photo reads: "Flying Service has Headquarters at St. Joseph County Airport. Homer Stockert relaxes at the wing of one of the planes available for chartering at Stockert Flying Service, Inc., located at the St. Joseph County Airport. The twin-engine aircraft is a Cessna 310, and the single-engine plane is a Cessna 210. These and three other planes are used for charter work. Stockert also has hangars, offices, a main office and lounge, a parts department and a shop. The business started in 1933." ("Air Service In Business Since 1933," *South Bend Tribune*, May 9, 1960: 14)

After the war, the Stockert Flying Service converted Vultee military aircraft to the specifications of a civilian airplane; some belonged to Chicago owners, some local.[5]

Homer and Dora continued to expand to meet new opportunities; their every step seemed newsworthy. In 1952, the Stockerts received approval to build an enlarged hangar at a cost of $100,000.

A Famed B-25 Bomber Roosts in Stockert's Hangar

Studebaker Corporation of South Bend was housing its executive DC-3 in Chicago, but now would hangar it close to home once the Stockert facility was available. In addition, the Bendix Corporation received permission from local authorities to conduct experiments with their B-25 two-engine WWII bomber maintained in a Stockert hangar.[6]

Qualified to fly multi-engine aircraft, Stockert flew the B-25 fitted with experimental Bendix brakes. Dora's niece, Ellen Simmons Ruppel, remembers watching Homer test the brakes:

> When I was about 12, Dora would take her sister, my sister, and I to her home in South Bend for a summer vacation. She would take us to their office at the airport. We would watch Homer testing the brakes on the B-25. They would run the airplane up and down the runway. They'd stop and make an adjustment on the brakes. Then they'd continue to taxi up and down a runway. It seemed so tedious. But it was all part of the Bendix process.[7]

Never letting the ups and downs of business alter his cheerful demeanor, Stockert was voted the "100 percent smiling pilot" at the South Bend airport.

The Stockert Flying Service flew Ralph J. Hennings, *Tribune* staff photographer, over Bendix Field in November 1958. The aerial panoramic shot of the field revealed how the population had grown along Lincolnway West in the vicinity of the airport in comparison to the farm land surrounding Bendix Field in 1945.[8] The Stockerts sold their ownership in the business in 1966 to David and John Farabough.

BEST SMILE

WINS CONTEST—Homer Stockert, winner of the smiles contest held recently at the South Bend airport. He was adjudged the "100 per cent smiling pilot."

The caption below the picture says it all!

Homer in an open cockpit, ready to serve with a smile.

In 1968, the *South Bend Tribune* ran an article on Bendix Field, by now referred to with a more geographic encompassing name as the St. Joseph County Airport. The paragraphs about the Stockert Flying Service emphasized the substantial status of its presence at the airport:

> Stockert Flying Service Inc., the oldest operator at the field, provides hangar space for approximately 100 corporate or private aircraft. This firm, which was founded by the pioneer flier, Homer Stockert, also operates a charter service and offers pilot instruction to the public as well as to University of Notre Dame Air reserve Officer Corps students. Stockert also is host to Business Fliers, an area organization of pilots who fly for business and pleasure. The group has 58 members with Roland I. Delcamp as president…"[9]

The caption of this photo reads: "Bird's Eye View of County Airport. The symmetrical pattern of runways at the St. Joseph County Airport is shown in this aerial view taken by Ralph J. Hennings, *Tribune* staff photographer, from a Stockert Flying Service plane. The top of the picture is north. The highway running diagonally across the scene in the foreground is Lincoln Way W. (U. S. 20). Just underneath the landing strips are the airport administration building and the entrance road going south to Lincoln Way." (*South Bend Tribune*, November 18, 1958)

Honored by His Home Town

The citizens of Churubusco, Indiana, took pride in their famous son and recognized his accomplishments on the back page of a program printed for the 15th annual National Convention of the OX5 Club of America that took place October 22-24, 1970, in Fort Wayne, Indiana. The tribute extolled his extraordinary achievements by proclaiming Stockert "Churubusco's most famous flying son and for his many contributions to aviation and to his fellow man."[10] One of the two photographs appearing on the page fittingly portrayed his professional career, featuring Homer standing on an airplane wheel holding his prize Studebaker loving cup (see page 11).

Chapter 9

Dora, the Glue for the Stockert Success

Also gifted with a winning smile, Dora managed a complex Stockert office. Their flying service offered nearly every function an airplane could provide. Student instructors, mechanics, parts department, sales, leased hangar space, and charter flights all created income and expenses requiring Dora's skill in organization and management. Homer brought in the business, but relied on Dora to run a tight ship. Ellen Ruppel recalls that Dora was very stern in dealings with the guys. A real take charge person. Homer smiled and went along.

Only once did Dora's niece, Ellen, see the two in a squabble:

> Homer sold a plane to another fellow with only an exchange of written statements. Homer wrote, "I sold this plane to [his name] for so much." The other fellow wrote, "I bought his plane from Homer Stockert for so much." They thought this exchange of signed letters was sufficient. Dora, as President and business manager of the Stockert Flying Service, was upset. The transaction should have been conducted with the legal papers she would have obtained from Wichita, Kansas. Dora was the business head of the couple. She could be stern when needed."[1]

The Stockerts incorporated: Dora, President; Homer, V.P.

Dora could cheerfully pose with Homer with a bi-wing in the background or grasp a wing spar of a WACO trainer.

But she didn't enjoy flying.

For some reason, Ellen remembered that Dora wore her hair differently as an adult than as a teenager.

Dora shared her artistic talents. She painted, carved small wooden statues, and made beautiful quilts. She gave one to her niece, Ellen, who has since donated it to a Ligonier museum.

Dora was not a fan of flying, despite her affection for her legendary pilot. Photo taken circa1941.

Even a legendary pilot failed to cajole Dora into learning how to fly. (Photo courtesy of the *South Bend Tribune*)

In the 1926 Junior Class, Churubusco, Indiana, Dora is in the second row, third from the left. She styled her hair to cover one eye. One eye was blue, the other brown. In high school, she was self conscious of the difference. In later years it didn't matter to her and she wore her hair away from her eyes (note the photos on page 77).

Gertrude Singer remembers Dora's generosity:

After receiving my certificate as an Air Traffic Controller in Chicago on August, 1943, and a brief stint as an instructor in the program, I was assigned to Bendix Field, Indiana. Late 1943, I arrived in South Bend on the South Shore and took a room in the Oliver Hotel. I had no idea where Bendix Field was but the taxi driver did and I arranged to arrive early the next day for work at the Bendix Control Tower. When I met the Chief Controller, I asked his advice about living accommodations in South Bend. He replied he didn't know, but he called Dora Stockert for her suggestions. Dora said, 'Send her over to me and she can stay with me for a while because Homer is not here.' And that's what happened. I went to her home. She had a nice house with an extra bedroom. Housing was tight during the war so I stayed there a few weeks until I could find my own apartment. I soon found out she was a good cook and loved to entertain. She was a lot of fun and she liked to play little jokes.

An example of Dora's ceramic work.

Small wooden smiling figurines carved by Dora. Their happy faces reflected Dora's personality.

Early on, I worked a midnight shift, so slept at Stockerts when not at the airport. I was fast asleep during the day and Dora was at work at the Stockert Flying Service. Homer was in Evansville as a test pilot for Republic Aviation. I heard voices downstairs. Two men were carrying a juke box into the basement. Thinking no one was home, they didn't spare their language as they wrestled the heavy player down the stairs. I poked my head down the stair well and saw two men. They were very embarrassed when they saw me. They introduced themselves and one was Julius Singer. Julius was from South Bend and Homer had taught him to fly. He then flew for Bendix Aviation testing equipment like aircraft brakes and carburetors.

The Stockerts and I were invited to Julius' apartment for a shrimp dinner, his specialty. He boiled them whole and served them in a big bowl on the table. There were small bowls with dips of butter or hot sauce. We would peel the shell off, place the shell in the empty bowl, dip the shrimp in a dip and eat it. Later when I was married to Julius, I happened to open the table drawer and found the dried out empty shells from the shrimp dinner. Dora had put them there for the fun of it.

Dora gave parties in their basement and invited people from the airport including Julius and me. I don't remember meeting any military types. A lot of combat aircraft

A Singer wedding picture taken on August 18, 1945, in front of the Stockert home in South Bend (L to R): Homer Stockert, Julius Singer, Gertrude Singer, and Dora Stockert. (Photo courtesy of Gertrude Reinders Singer)

flew into Bendix Field and the military serviced them at the east end of the field at the Indiana Flying Service. Homer got all the civilian traffic. Homer came home from Evansville when Julius and I were married. Homer and Dora stood up for us at our church wedding. Julius and Homer were good friends.

Dora was a lot of fun but also a very good business woman. She could keep good records so she ended up running the business.[2]

Chapter 10
Setting Sun on the Stockert Dream

Homer, an avid sportsman, enjoyed both fishing and hunting.

By 1965, Homer was 66 and had spent a full life, often opening the office early in the morning and locking up late at night. Bill Hite, Ellen's cousin, recounted a story about a state trooper and then ended it with an observation about Homer's health:

> We'd been down goose hunting. We came up to Kankakee. The closer we came to South Bend, the faster he would drive. Just about a mile from the hangar, the red light came on. The state trooper came up and said, "Let's see your pilot's license." Homer had his and gave it to the trooper. The trooper said, "Well you got me there. I often ask for a pilot's license when I catch

Duck for dinner at the Stockerts?

With his airplanes, Homer could easily fly to the ocean to enjoy deep sea fishing. Ellie Ruppel: "Dora used to go on the fishing trips. But then she quit. Wasn't any fun because she had to do all the cooking."

Homer tends to his pack of puppies.

Christmas dinner, 1964; Homer playfully holding two grandnieces.

> people driving fast, and you're the first one that had one." After that, Homer said, "Don't tell Dora." I said, "OK, I won't." But by the next year, he'd drive a while and then he'd ask me to drive. He was getting confused.[1]

August 23, 1965, Homer flew for the last time. He spent his remaining days caring for his beloved springer spaniels and spending time with his extended family.

His health slipping away, Homer died January 12, 1971. The laudatory review of Homer's life in his obituary summed up his career with "Short, stocky, genial and grinning, Stockert was an aviation booster and a legend in his own time."[2]

Dora continued to work at the Stockert Flying Service, bearing the new name SBN Aviation, Inc. In 1982, Dora was recognized for her contribution and help in the development of aviation and various individuals whom she and Homer helped launch their careers in the flying business at Bendix Field. The title of the article about the occasion read, "Dinner honors Dora Stockert, grand lady of local aviation."[3]

Dora passed away fifteen years later. An inscription on their headstone, "Together Forever," captured their love for one another.

During their lifetime, both Homer and Dora received deserved recognition for their contributions to a fledgling innovation called aviation, as well as to the young men and women intrigued with piloting and the business elements of such a promising invention. This story endeavors to reflect that greatness.

Dora is recognized for her contributions to local aviation.

NEW FLYING SERVICE — Owners of South Bend's newest flying service at the Michiana Regional Airport thank Dora Stockert, seated second from left, for her assistance in starting their new service. The new owners of the former Stockert Flying Service are, from left; Michael Krueger, Ralph Kern and Philip McClure.

Tribune Staff Photo by Ron Ryback

SOUTH BEND TRIBUNE - JANUARY 10, 1982

Dinner honors Dora Stockert, grand lady of local aviation

South Bend's newest general aviation flying service, SBN Aviation, Inc., owes much to Dora Stockert, the grand lady of aviation in the area.

The new owners of the former Stockert Flying Service at the Michiana Regional Airport said it was her willingness to "give us a helping hand" that caused them to succeed in aviation.

"We owe a debt of gratitude to Dora Stockert," said Phillip McClure, one of the SBN Aviation principals.

Mrs. Stockert, and her late husband, Homer, helped them all to get started in the aviation field, said McClure, who also is owner and operator of Ni-Cad Inc., helicopter services at the airport.

McClure, Michael Krueger and Ralph Kern are principal owners of SBN Aviation, Inc., the newly formed aviation firm that purchased the foundering Stockert operation.

Krueger is manager of Kern's Aviation Electroncis, Inc., and Kern is a former owner of the Kern's firm.

McClure, Krueger and Kern and their wives Friday night honored Mrs. Stockert at a dinner at the Marriott Hotel.

Mrs. Stockert continued to work for several years at Stockert's Flying Service after her husband died in 1971.

Her work at the flying service has made her known to most of the pilots in the area for the last 50 years.

McClure said he came here as a mechanic for the Associates Corp. jet craft about 10 years ago and Mrs. Stockert made it possible for him to obtain his flying licenses.

Krueger started in aviation as a flight line worker for Stockert's and moved up the aviation ladder by becoming chief pilot and general manager for Stockert's.

Kern began the aviation electronic service and was assisted along the way by the Stockerts.

SBN Aviation currently is leasing hangars owned by the airport but in a few years will move to new hangars to be constructed on the north edge of the airport, said McClure.

Together Forever: Homer and Dora rest in peace in Highland Park Cemetery, Portage Road, South Bend, Indiana.

TABLE I : Army Air Corps Commanding Officers At Bendix Field (names may not be in chronological order)	
Capt. William E. Dillon	July 13,1943 to June 21, 1944
Major Lloyd M. Graves	June 21, 1944 to -
Lt. W. J. Pennington	1945

Table II : List of Service Personnel Stationed At Bendix Field March 1944

Adkins, Joe W., Pfc.
Arnett, Orval K., Sgt.
Banks, Woodrow, Pvt.
Barron, John A., Pfc.
Barton, Harold G., Cpl.
Batterson, Miles F., 2/Lt.
Bird, James H., Jr., Cpl.
Blank, Leo A., S/Sgt.
Bottler, Raymond E., Cpl.
Brady, Paul H., Cpl.
Brody, Martin, Sgt.
Budukiewicz, John V., 1/Lt.
Burkey, Bernard E., Cpl.
Campesie, Augustine, Pfc.
Carlson, John D., Sgt.
Carroll, Robert W., Pfc.
Cofield, Paul H., Cpl.
Cook, Allen, Pvt.
Cottrell, Donald J., Cpl.
DeLaVegne, Leroy M., Cpl.
Dillon, William E., Capt.
DiJoseph, Frank, Pfc.
Donham, Robert A., Sgt.
Dykstra, Bernard, Pvt.
English, Cecil H., 1/Lt.
Falco, Michael, Sgt.
Flanegan, Richard F., Cpl.
Fliedner, William L., Cpl.
Freeman, George W., Pvt.
Frierson, Laurance W., Capt.
Gialanella, Joseph A., Jr., Cpl.
Graves, Lloyd M., Maj..
Guillemette, Louis M., Pfc.
Hamel, Elmer A., Cpl.
Hardy, William C., Pfc.
Heginbotham, James, L., Cpl.
Hynes, Eugene, S/Sgt.
Johnson, Arling H., Lt.
Johnson, David L., Pfc.
Keith, John A., Cpl.
Kennedy, Louis A., Pfc.
Kopp, Charles H., Sgt.
Kraus, James S., Cpl.
Lackey, George H., T/Sgt.
Lee, Johnney B., Pvt.
Lee, Walter J., S/Sgt.
Limeburner, Russell M., Pvt.
Macy, Marvin D., Cpl.
Mandt, Frederick, W., Sgt.
Marano, Raymond C., Cpl.
Matthews, LeRoy, 1/Sgt.
McDonough, Henry L., Cpl.
McMillin, Bert M., 1/Lt.
Morreale, James V., Pvt.
Neighbarger, Joe D., Cpl.
Nelson, William H., Jr., Cpl.
Nelson, William T., Jr., Pfc.
Norman, Orville G., Pfc.
Parker, Stewart S., Pvt.
Pennington, Willis, 1/Lt.
Peshia, Wilbur, L., WOJC
Plesnicher, Paul F., CWO
Pratt, Oral, Sgt.
Radford, William C., Pfc.
Randolph, Edgar E., Sgt.
Rathbunn, Perry W., Sgt.
Routsaw, Joseph C., Pfc.
Russman, James D., Cpl.
Samars, Peter, Pvt.
Schenk, Norbert R., 1/Lt.
Simons, Ralph N., Pfc.
Slate, Sherwood, Cpl.
Scott, Sterling P., Sgt.
Shelton, George M., S/Sgt.
Stubblefield, Bill J., Pfc.
Vaught, Donald, Pfc.
Vieau, Earl J., Cpl.
Vogel, Edward J., Pfc.
Wallschlaeger, Theodore W., 2/Lt.
Walter, William H., Pfc.
Weibel, George M., 1/Lt.
Williams, Franklin B., Pfc.

(from Special Orders 30 March 1944, 2/Lt. Miles F. Batterson, courtesy of Margery Batterson)

Table III : Military Aircraft Accidents at or Near Bendix Field

Major Accident

One Mile North of Bendix Field

The Boeing P-26C was the first all-metal monoplane accepted by the Army Air Corps as a pursuit fighter. Called the "Peashooter" by the pilots, it was armed with two fixed .30 or .50 caliber machine guns and capable of carrying up to 200 pounds in bombs. Its top speed was 234mph. (Photo courtesy of Wikipedia)

July 18, 1937. Pilot: 2/Lt. Robert A. Theobald, Air Reserve, assigned to Selfridge Field, Michigan. Aircraft: P-26C #33-196. At 1p.m. July 18th, Lt. Theobald took off from Bendix Field for a navigation training flight to Selfridge Field. At an altitude of 2,700 feet one mile north of Bendix Field, Roberts began to perform a variety of stunt maneuvers. After several rolls, his plane failed to recover from a snap roll, stalled on its back, and entered into a downward inverted spin. The pilot managed to stop the inverted spin when the plane developed a normal spin. The pilot was unable to escape the spin, and at an altitude of 600 feet, Theobald parachuted from the plane and landed safely. The plane continued downward and crashed on land owned by Eduard Cornwall, RD3, Box 8, South Bend, Indiana. Mr. Cornwall asserted the plane caused no damage to his property.

Because the plane had been loaded with a full capacity of fuel in its auxiliary tanks, safety procedures stated for this plane when loaded to its heaviest weight prohibited stunt flying. The investigating committee from Selfridge Field, Michigan, concluded the accident was due to 100% pilot error. (AFHRA: Call: Mf: 46040, IRIS: 876987)

Minor Accident

At Bendix Field

The Bell P-39 in flight. The Aircobra proved a ground attack fighter armed with one 37mm cannon firing through the nose and six machine guns firing from the fuselage and wings. (Photo courtesy of Wikipedia)

May 4, 1943. Pilot: 1/Lt. Edmond J. Arbib, assigned to Air Transport Command, Romulus AFB, Michigan. Aircraft: P-39-N5-BE #42-18943. Pilot was cleared from Buffalo, New York, to Bendix Field. In landing at Bendix Field, the pilot dropped the plane about ten feet to the runway. The plane landed hard on the left wheel, then bounced up and came down again hard on the right wheel. The violent contact with the runway caused damage to both wing assemblies, all three tricycle landing gears, and the fuselage. The pilot asserted the landing incident was not due to a civilian aircraft being too close to the runway. Captain F. D. Ely, Bendix Field Servicing Detachment, stated the plane may have hindered the landing. (AFHRA: Call: Mf: 46198)

Minor Accident

At a Field Outside South Bend

June 6, 1943. Pilot: Flight Officer (F/O) James W. Metsker, assigned to ATC, Nashville, Tennessee. Aircraft: PT 26A #42-70996. Metsker was cleared from Bendix Field to Madison, Wisconsin, on a ferrying mission. About two miles west of Bendix Field, his engine began to pound as if due to a lost bearing. He made an emergency landing in a field and was not injured. The Servicing Detachment at Bendix Field hauled the plane back to the field and determined the motor would have to be replaced. (AFHRA Mf: 46212)

The Fairchild PT (Primary Trainer)-26 Cornell was the trainer aircraft utilized by the United States Army Air Corps, the Royal Canadian Air Force, and the Royal Air Force. It was used to first introduce a flying cadet to flying. Its top speed was 132mph. (Photo courtesy of NMUSAF)

Major Accident

At Bendix Field

June 24, 1943. Pilot: 2/Lt. George W. Fairchild III, assigned to Romulus Army Air Base, Michigan. Aircraft: PT-26 #42-71014. A flight of five PT-26s was taking off from Bendix Field in a flight to Madison, Wisconsin. Fairchild was third in line to take off. His run-up of his engine was normal. He began his take-off when plane 2 was airborne. He applied throttle and began to gain speed. Halfway down the runway, he noted the plane was not achieving adequate speed; even full power did not increase his speed. To avoid crashing through a fence and field lights, he pulled up at the end of the runway, became airborne for about 150 feet, flew over the fence, then stalled and slammed into the ground. He was not injured, but considerable damage was done to the plane. Inspection of the engine revealed that the rod between the throttle and the carburetor was so loose that full power could not be achieved. (AFHRA Mf: 46218)

Minor Accident

At Bendix Field

July 25, 1943. Pilot: 1/Lt. Albert J. Dryden, assigned to ATC, Nashville, Tennessee. Plane: P-39-Q5 #42-20374. The pilot planned to fly locally in an effort to determine the cause of oil loss in the engine during a flight from Detroit. The pilot took off at 12:50p.m., flew about South Bend for 50 minutes, then came in for a landing. The investigating team reported that at about 10 feet above the end of the runway, the motor stalled, causing the plane to drop hard onto the runway. After a short roll, the nose wheel began to retract, resulting in the propeller striking the hardened runway. The nose landing gear, tires, propeller drive shaft, and engine were damaged as a result. Examining the control panel in the parked aircraft, they noted that the landing gear toggle switch was in the "up" position. Yet, the pilot stated that he had lowered the landing gear. The investigating team concluded that the hard landing may have jarred the flexibly-mounted instrument panel and consequently the landing gear toggle switch into the "up" position. (AFHRA Mf: 46231)

Minor Accident

At Bendix Field

February 5, 1944. Pilot: 2/Lt. C. P. McClanahan, assigned to ATC, Great Falls, Montana. Aircraft: P-40N #43-23242. He was conducting a ferrying mission. McClanahan landed normally and was following a parking jeep when his right wheel sank into a hole in the soft mud, causing the plane to pivot and nose up so that the propeller struck the ground; damage was restricted to the propeller only. The motor was not damaged. Capt. William Dillon, Commandant of the Servicing Detachment, took the blame for the accident for ordering planes to be parked in the muddy area. He appealed to his superiors to provide a hard surface in the parking areas. (AFHRA Mf. 46320)

The Curtiss P-40, manufactured by the Curtiss Aircraft Company, Buffalo, NY, first saw combat flown by British pilots in North Africa in 1940. A total of 13,700 were built, with many flown by other Allied nations. (Photo courtesy of NMUSAF)

Major Accident

At Bendix Field

March 6, 1945. Pilot: Capt. James J. Dormer; Co-Pilot: 1/Lt. Charles M. Evans; T/Sgt. John E. Lynch, Crew Chief; and Cpl. Thomas Moore, Assistant Crew Chief, all assigned to Olmsted Field, Middletown, Pennsylvania. Aircraft: C-47B, #43-16157. Passenger: Col. George G. Cressey. The C-47 was flown from Olmsted Field to pick up cargo from the 820th Specialized Depot, South Bend, Indiana, and return to Olmsted Field. While the plane was being loaded a light to moderate snow fell, covering both wings. Captain Dormer sent Lynch and Moore to clean the snow off the wings before take off, then the plane was taxied to the west end of runway 5, heading northeast, and began an eleven-minute run-up of the engines. The wind was blowing snow from the north; thus, snow began to accumulate on the left wing but not the right wing, which was protected by the C-47 fuselage. As the plane began take-off, the right wheel left the runway but the left wheel did not. The left wing had lost lift because of the weight of the snow and the fact that the snow spoiled the airfoil of the wing, eliminating its lift. Unable to become airborne, the pilot shut down the engines, but too late. The plane ran off the runway, traveled across a road, and smashed into three fences, a telephone pole, and several small trees. Both propellers, landing gear, engines, fuselage, and vertical fin were all severally damaged. No personnel were injured. The investigating team concluded that no plane should attempt take-off with any accumulation of snow or ice on the wings. (AAIR)

The Douglas C-47 Skytrain proved a multitask weapon capable of duties, such as transporting paratroopers, gunship, air ambulance, and cargo ship. (Photo courtesy of Wikipedia)

Major Accident-Fatal

1½ Miles Northwest of South Bend, Indiana

May 12, 1945. Pilot: 2/Lt. Frederick H. Edwards; navigator 1/Lt. Julius Goldstein; navigator 1/Lt. Barnard M. Plaut; navigator 1/Lt. Frank A. Picard; and engineer Joseph M. Adragna. Aircraft: AT-7 #42-2478. The plane left Chicago Municipal Airport at 10:17 p.m. on a flight to Bendix Field. Observers sighted the plane flying north over the field at an altitude of about 400 feet heading north. Beginning a left turn to enter the traffic pattern, it was lost from sight as it entered a fog bank. Moments later, personnel at the field heard a crash. The plane had smashed into the ground one and a half miles north of Bendix Field. Edwards, Goldstein, and Plaut were killed; Picard and Adragna suffered only minor injuries. The survivors believed the crash was due to a faulty altimeter. (Anthony J. Mireles, *Fatal Army Air Forces Aviation Accidents in the United States, 1941-1945*, vol.3: August 1944-December 1945, McFarland & Co., Jefferson, NC, 1963: 1095)

Minor Accident

At Bendix Field

September 9, 1945. Pilot: 1/Lt. Willie E. Brinkman, assigned to Dover AFB, Delaware. Aircraft: P-47 #44-87940. The mission was a weekend cross country flight. Brinkman arrived in South Bend, then attempted to receive permission to continue on to Chicago. Permission was denied due to poor weather conditions over Chicago, so Brinkman decided to land. He achieved a normal three-point landing, but after a roll of about 800 feet, his left brake seemed to grab when he applied the brakes. When the plane slowed, braking caused the nose to drop and the prop struck the runway; only the propeller was damaged. No damage was done to the motor. After the accident, the brake actions were found to be normal. The investigating team surmised the accident was caused by excessive braking by the pilot. (Air Force Historical Studies Office, Bolling AFB, DC. "P-47 Noses Over At Airport Here Pilot Uninjured," *South Bend Tribune*, September 9, 1945:12)

The Republic P-47 Thunderbolt, weighing in at 9+ tons was the heaviest U. S. fighter in WWII. Francis Gabreski, a leading ace, flew only the P-47, a testimony to its prowess in the skies. (Photo courtesy of Ellie Ruppel)

Air Force Historical Research Agency microfilm, Maxwell AFB, AL (AFHRA); National Museum of the United States Air Force, Wright-Patterson AFB, OH (NMUSAF); Aviationarchaeology.com (AAIR) (Photo may be a variant of the aircraft)

Chapter 11:
Bendix Field to South Bend International

St. Joseph County Airport Authority is currently the owner and manager of South Bend International Airport, formerly known as Bendix field. As stated by the current Director of Marketing and Development, Julie Curtis:

> South Bend International Airport (SBN) currently offers nonstop service to nine destinations on three carriers: Delta daily to Atlanta, Detroit, and Minneapolis; United daily to Chicago; and Allegiant to Fort Myers/Punta Gorda, Las Vegas, Orlando/Sanford, Phoenix/Mesa, and Tampa/St. Petersburg. Because SBN is close and convenient to the entire Northern Indiana/Southwestern Michigan region, travelers avoid the traffic headaches and additional costs often found when using larger airports in other cities. Parking is close and inexpensive, and additional transportation services—taxis, rental cars, buses and trains—get you to your final destination with ease. With an abundance of time and money-saving advantages including free WiFi and exceptional customer service, SBN is ideal for getting you anywhere you need to go. You are just one stop from wherever your travels take you.

South Bend International Airport (SBN) as it appears today.

Endnotes

Chapter 1

1. "Flies 3,500 Hours With Not A Scratch"*
2. "Meet Our Fliers"—Homer Stockert.
3. "Stockert Test Pilot for P-47 Fighter Plane," *South Bend Tribune*, October 1, 1943.
4. "Thousands Mourn Stockert," *South Bend Tribune*, January 14, 1971.

"Infant Dies After Short Illness"

5. "Meet Our Fliers"—Homer Stockert.
6. "Meet Our Fliers"—Homer Stockert.
7. "2 Local Youths Win Prizes In Air Meet," May 20, 1928.
8. "Meet Our Fliers"—Homer Stockert.
9. Roberts, Rachel S., *Art Smith: Pioneer Aviator*. McFarland & Company, Inc., Publishers, Jefferson, North Carolina, 2003, pg. 152
6. Winebrenner Family History, http://www.winebrenner.net/PAF_Data/pafn03.htm
7. "Four Are Killed In Air Collision," *Pittsburgh Post-Gazette*, September 13, 1937: 2; "Butz Enters Plane in Chicago Races, *South Bend Tribune*, July 2, 1933, Section 4:2.
8. "Aviation Field For South Bend Is Now Assured," *South Bend Tribune*, July, 1930.
9. "Field Adjacent To City Limits Hits Civic Port," *South Bend News Times*, March 17, 1931, Part 2: 1.
10. "Liners Flying U.S. Will Stop At Bendix Port," *South Bend Tribune*, June 18, 1931.
11. "Radio Beam Will Triple Air Traffic," *South Bend Tribune*, September 22, 1938.

Chapter 2

1. "Race Pilots Win $925 in Prizes At Port Opening," *Defiance Crescent News*, September 4, 1928: 1.
2. Sarah Lockerbie, "He Taught the Girls to Fly," *South Bend Tribune Magazine*, February 10, 1957: 8.
3. "Test pilot De Munck: He came to expect the unexpected," *South Bend Tribune, Michiana Section*, January 18, 1987.
4. Lewis McCombs's communication to the author.
5. "Thousands View Spectacular Flight Of Graf Zeppelin As It Passes Near City," *South Bend Tribune, Second Section*, August 29, 1929: 3.

Chapter 3

1. Dary Matera, *John Dillinger: The Life and Death of America's First Celebrity Criminal*. Carroll & Graf Publishers, New York, 2004. pg. 320.
2. "Air Service in Business Since 1933," *South Bend Tribune*, May 9, 1960: 14.

Chapter 4

1. "Gabreski," *Air Force Magazine* vol. 88, No. 11, November 2005.
2. ibid. Chapter 1, ref. 6.
3. Microfilm #46375, IRIS: 877322, AFHRA, Maxwell AFB, Alabama.

* All newspaper clippings lacking origin are in the possession of Ellen Rippel.

4. "Stockert Tops 12,000 Flying Hours," *Republic Aviation News, Indiana Division*, March 9, 1945.
5. Microfilm #46413, IRIS No. 877360, AFHRA, Maxwell AFB, Alabama.
6. Report of Aircraft Accident, Genovese/ Cushman, 3 May 1944. Accident-Report. com, Millville, New Jersey 08332.
7. Microfilm #46338, IRIS No. 877285, AFHRA, Maxwell, AFB, Alabama.
8. ibid. ref. 4.

Chapter 5

1. "South Bend May Build Field For Airmail Planes," *South Bend News-Times*, July 22, 1927.
2. "South Bend's Progress Needs Airport Facility," *South Bend Tribune*, September 18, 1927.
3. "Council Authorizes Purchase of Municipal Airport for South Bend," *South Bend News-Times*, June 27, 1928: 1, and Editorial, "The City's Airport," page 6.
4. "South Bend Port Mecca For Ships," *South Bend News-Times*, March 21, 1928:Part 2.
5. "Plane Brings Local Residents to City", *South Bend News-Times*, April 24, 1928: 4.
6. "Youths Enlist For Plane Show," *South Bend News-Times*, April 26, 1928, part 2: 1.
7. "Pilots Enter 30 Planes for South Bend's Air Meet," *South Bend News-Times*, May 18, 1928: 1.
8. "Pretty Air Queen Entrant," *South Bend News-Times*, May 6, 1928: 12.
9. "Huge Throng Attends Elaborate Ceremonies at Dedication of Airport," *South Bend News-Times*, May 20, 1928: 1.
10. "More Than 20,000 Attend Closing Day of Air Meet," *South Bend News-Times*, May 21, 1928: 1.
11. "Plane Brings Movietone News to City," *The South Bend News-Times*, August 2, 1928: 4; "Planes Zoom City As Meet Begins," *South Bend Tribune*, September 15, 1928: 1; "Daredevil Airmen Thrill South Bend," *South Bend Tribune*, September 16, 1928, Magazine Section; "Giant Air Meet Attended By 30,000," *South Bend Tribune*, September 17, 1928, Second Section.
12. Rebecca Wolfe, p. 6.
13. "Thousands On Hand To See Aerial Feats," *The South Bend Tribune*, September 5, 1933. 9; The Bendix Trophy pamphlet, Bendix Aerospace, 1000 Wilson Boulevard, Arlington, VA, 22209.
14. ibid.

Chapter 6

1. "TWA May Put Airport Here On Schedule," *South Bend Tribune*, July 23, 1940; "2 Routes Amended To Include Stop At South Bend." Civil Aeronautics Journal, Air Transportation, December 15, 1941: 318.
2. *South Bend Tribune*, December 1939.
3. "St. Joseph County Archives" (R1 Commissioners Record), Vol. 29, January 1940-December 1942, South Bend, Indiana.
4. Communication from Jack Saylor to the author.
5. Communication from Gertrude Singer to the author, June 2005.
6. "Survey of Premises," St. Joseph Co. Archives, R1, Commissioners Record, Vol. 29, January 1940 to December 1942: November 16, 1942; "Army Will Give Up $7,000,000 Superairport," *South Bend Tribune*, August 11, 1943.
7. "Army To Curb Port Activity Here On Aug. 20," *South Bend Tribune*, July 27, 1945.
8. Call: 301.073-1, IRIS: 00180421 and 00180422, AFHRA, Maxwell AFB, AL.

9. "Air Base Head Entertains 300," *South Bend Tribune*, January 3, 1945: 1.
10. "Air Ace Back From Pacific Permanently," *South Bend Tribune,* January 10, 1945: Section 2.
11. " Mayor Urges City Mark Air Force Day," *South Bend Tribune,* July 27, 1945.

Chapter 7

1. Call:* 00402, IRIS 31704, AFHRA, Maxwell AFB, Alabama.
2. Call: 206.820-1 V.2, IRIS143322; call: 206.820-4, IRIS 143324; call: 206.820-5, IRIS 143325; call: 206.820-9, IRIS: 143329; call: 205.02-1A, IRIS 142527, AFHRA, Maxwell AFB, Alabama.
3. "Air Force Depot Here Adopts Plan To Combat Absenteeism," *South Bend Tribune*, January 31, 1945.

Chapter 8

1. "Pilot Training Proves Popular," *South Bend Tribune*, June 16, 1946: 15.
2. "War Vets Begin Flight Training," *South Bend Tribune*, June 10, 1946: 9.
3. ibid. Chapter 1, Endnote 2.
4. "Plane Repair Exacting Work," *South Bend Tribune*, December 30, 1947, Section 2: 1.
5. "Military Planes Converted To Private Service," *South Bend Tribune*, July 5, 1946, Section 2: 1.
6. "Airport Firm Plans Hangar," *South Bend Tribune*, September 7, 1952.
7. Communication from Ellen Ruppel to the author, April 4, 2006.
8. "Bird's Eye View of County Airport," *South Bend Tribune*, November 18, 1958, Section 2: 1.
9. "St. Joseph Airport Receives Many Types," *South Bend Tribune*, November 17, 1968, Michiana Sunday Magazine.
10. "A Tribute to...HOMER S. STOCKERT From Many of His Hometown Friends In Churubusco, Indiana," 15th Annual National Convention of OX5 Club of America, October 22-23-24, 1970, Baer Field Inn, Fort Wayne, Indiana.

Chapter 9

1. Communication from Ellen Ruppel to the author.
2. Communication from Gertrude Singer to the author.

Chapter 10

1. Taped communication with Bill Hite and the author.
2. "Thousands Morn Stockert," *South Bend Tribune*, January 14, 1971.
3. "Dinner honors Dora Stockert, grand lady of local aviation," *South Bend Tribune*, January 10, 1982: 19.

* Call refers to the digital search term that accompanies the unit history at Maxwell AFB.

Index